TURNED
TOYS

TURNED
TOYS

MARK BAKER

The Taunton Press

The Taunton Press
Inspiration for hands-on living®

The Taunton Press, Inc., 63 South Main Street, P.O. Box 5506, Newtown, CT 06470-5506

e-mail: tp@taunton.com

First published 2016 by

Guild of Master Craftsman Publications Ltd

Castle Place, 166 High Street

Lewes, East Sussex, BN7 1XU

Publisher: Jonathan Bailey

Production Manager: Jim Bulley

Senior Project Editor: Sara Harper

Managing Art Editor: Gilda Pacitti

Designer: Ali Walper

Photographer: Anthony Bailey

Drawings: Mark Carr

Library of Congress Cataloging-in-Publication Data

Names: Baker, Mark, 1966- author.

Title: Turned toys / Mark Baker.

Description: Newtown, CT : The Taunton Press, Inc., 2016. | Includes index.

Identifiers: LCCN 2016021953 | ISBN 9781631866531

Subjects: LCSH: Wooden toy making. | Turning (Lathe work)

Classification: LCC TT174.5.W6 B32 2016 | DDC 745.592--dc23

LC record available at https://lccn.loc.gov/2016021953

Set in Merriweather and ClanPro

Color origination by GMC Reprographics

Printed and bound in China

CONTENTS

HEDGEHOGS
28

SPINNING TOP
58

**WOODEN
PUZZLE**
34

MONEY BOX
40

PENGUIN SKITTLES
66

LIGHTHOUSE STACKER
48

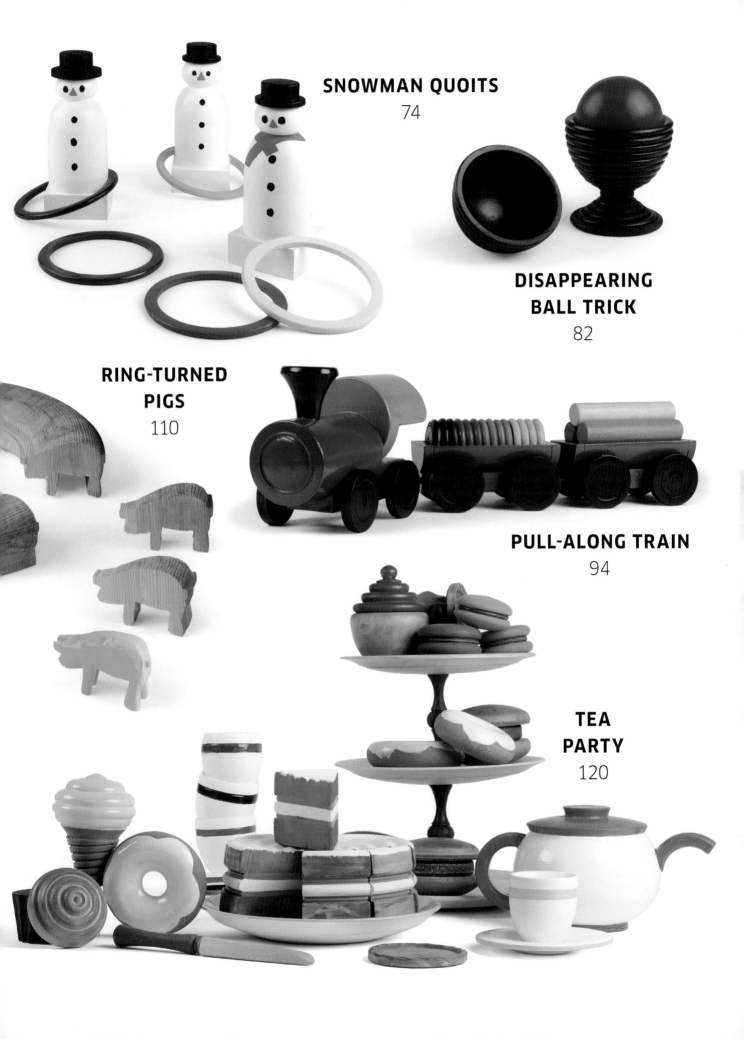

Introduction

In this age of mass-production we see fewer and fewer homemade toys. It is, of course, true that homemade electronic toys are not always viable, but what about the traditional toys that we played with as children? They have not lost their fun factor. We loved them when we were young, and I'm certain that their appeal has stood the test of time. There is also something rather wonderful about giving a homemade toy as a gift, while making it yourself also offers the opportunity to involve your children and grandchildren in helping with the choice of design and decoration.

This book is intended to appeal to turners who are looking for projects that will help them to develop their turning skills, while at the same time creating something for their children and grandchildren to enjoy. It will also stir nostalgia in the bigger children at home. The book includes 20 projects for toys and tricks of various types. I will show you how to create the parts and pieces for games such as quoits and skittles, which the whole family can get involved in – indoors and outdoors, whatever the weather.

Due to limitations of space, I am not able to spend much time on basic instructions for using tools, so have had to assume that the reader knows the fundamentals for using core equipment. That said, I do offer guidance along with helpful hints and tips for tools and techniques that might be unfamiliar or not commonly encountered.

The projects are designed to create toys that are bright, colorful and tactile. They are toys, tricks and games that encourage children to learn skills while they use and play with them. These include motor skills, hand–eye coordination, information processing and creativity, but children won't feel as though they're being taught because they'll be having too much fun! Hopefully, you'll be enjoying yourself just as much, and developing your own woodturning skills, when making the toys.

The Basics

Toy safety

Homemade toys for personal use are not subject to legislation, but you should research good safety standards and learn from the advice and information that is available online. That way, you can create toys that are both fun and safe for children to play with.

There is a good deal of legislation on the subject of making toys and toy safety, and each country has its own laws. These are aimed at manufacturers making toys for sale. Different laws address such considerations as materials, design, age of user, size of items, finish, chemical composition of components and stress tests.

The first thing for you to consider is the age of the child who will be playing with the toy. The toy being made needs to be of an age-appropriate size and weight. Also, if a toy is being made for use by a child under three years of age, then there is the danger that small items may be put in the mouth and chewed. If any part of the toy is less than 1¼in. (32mm) in diameter, then it represents a potential choke hazard. Spheres or balls under 1¾in. (45mm) in diameter may also be dangerous, even for older children. Choke hazards are a very serious thing, so do consider them carefully. You can buy a choke test cylinder from various sources or make your own to the relevant patterns available on the internet, which provides a quick and easy way to assess the hazards presented by different parts.

Materials must be suitable for their intended purpose. There should be no sharp points or edges, easily broken parts, or items prone to fracturing or splintering. Finishes should be toy safe. Each toy should also be of a size and weight suitable for the intended age group. Common sense and a little bit of research should provide you with a framework within which to work. Searching the internet for 'toy safety legislation' will help you to find lots of helpful information. Always check, check again, and err on the side of caution. If in doubt, change something to make sure you are happy that all risks have been minimized or removed completely.

Dangers with toys

A couple of examples demonstrate how toys might be considered dangerous for very young children. In the case of the Spinning Top project (see page 58), there is a cord attached to a small handle, creating a strangulation risk for the cord and a choke hazard for the handle. These considerations make the toy unsuitable for children under three years of age. The Knife (see page 160), which is one of the many projects in the Tea Party section, is long and thin, so it also presents a potential choking hazard for very young children. When making toys for children, be guided by legislation but also use your common sense.

Equipment

This book assumes that the reader owns a chuck, mounting accessories and common workshop equipment, and the projects require a basic knowledge of turning.

LATHES

Whether you use a variable-speed lathe or a manual belt-change lathe is up to you. I would say that the variable-speed ones, although costing more, do make things a little easier and give you more options in terms of speed. A few revs up or down at times can help minimize vibration.

Lathes come in all shapes and sizes, to suit all workshop areas and sizes of project. I have designed all the projects to be created on a lathe with a 14-in. (350mm) swing and 18 in. (460mm) between centers. That said, in reality a 12-in. (300mm) swing will work for all but one of the projects. The Ring-turned pig (see page 110) is better suited to the bigger lathe, but even that can be tackled by using a smaller diameter log than the one featured. Of course, you can always choose to use a bigger lathe, but these are invariably more expensive.

Whatever lathe you are using, make sure that it is placed on a sturdy bench to support it, or is securely fixed to a purpose-built stand. The heavier and more sturdy the stand or bench, the better you will find the vibration-dampening qualities.

Record Power DML 305 lathe.

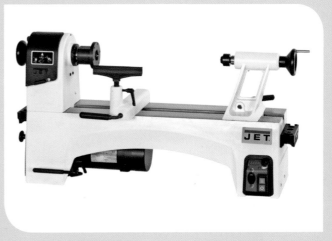

Jet JWL-1221VS lathe.

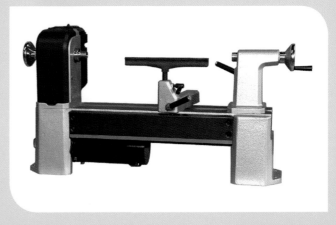

Delta 46-460 lathe.

CHUCKS, DRIVES AND CENTERS

I have made the assumption that readers will use a chuck. Most turners use them these days, and they do make life easier. There are numerous chucks and work-mounting accessories available. The projects in the book require a basic scroll, or geared, chuck – 4 in. (100mm), or close to this, is ideal – with a set of dovetail- or gripper-type jaws that can lock down onto a spigot (or tenon) of a maximum 2⅝ in. (67mm). A little more capacity than this is helpful, but not essential.

The key with using spigots is to have as large a size as possible, to increase stability without compromising your ability to shape the work. Too small a spigot in relation to the size of the work means the piece will not be supported properly while it is being cut. This increases the risk of breaking the spigot, especially on faceplate-orientated grain. Chucks are often supplied with a screw chuck as standard equipment or as an optional accessory. If you do not have one, a faceplate can be used instead.

Like chucks, drives and centers come in all shapes and sizes. For these projects, a standard two- or four-prong drive will suffice along with a standard point revolving center. I typically use a combination of a point and ring center. The ring center is the one I use the most, as it spreads the bearing load over a larger area. It also allows me more easily to reverse friction-drive work for finishing off a base, and minimizes the risk of splitting the small stub of wood that is left.

Clockwise from top left: faceplates, chucks, revolving centers, screw chuck inserts and drives.

Tools and materials

I use a basic set of turning tools, and the sizes shown in the picture of the basic set are suitable for the projects in this book. Your choice of tools is key to shaping your work, but there are so many available that it can become confusing. Here, I present a quick guide to the essentials.

PARTING TOOLS AND SCRAPERS

The tool sizes shown here make an ideal starter set. You can get larger or smaller, but you should only add to the set when you need to. If you decide to use a bigger lathe, you may find that you need to have some bigger bowl and spindle gouges, for instance, to tackle bigger and deeper work. The sizes shown here, though, are an excellent starting point.

When it comes to parting tools, there are many to choose from, ranging from about $1/16$ in. (1.5mm) upwards. For versatility I would recommend that you have two parting tools. First, a beading and parting tool, typically $3/8$ in. (10mm) wide, for big cuts, waste removal and cutting beads. Second, you should have a deep-bladed, thin parting tool, about $5/64$–$1/8$ in. (2–3mm) wide, for delicate cuts and minimizing waste. In one of the projects I use a different one, $1/4$ in. (6mm) wide, but this is for one cut and the beading and parting tool would also work, albeit at a slower pace. If you were only to buy one parting tool, the most versatile one would be the $1/4$ in. (6mm) thin parting tool.

I also use scrapers. These are used to refine a surface after shaping has been done with a gouge. There are a couple of routes you can follow. The first route is to use conventional rectangular scrapers with shaped ends – a French curve for internal curves, and either a square-across or angled cutting edge for external curves. You can introduce a third type of end if you wish, with a shallow curvature on the front, for slow, shallow internal curves.

From left to right: $3/4$-in. (20mm) spindle roughing gouge, $3/8$-in (10mm) bowl gouge, $1/2$-in. (13mm) spindle gouge, $3/8$-in. (10mm) spindle gouge, $3/4$-in. (20mm) skew chisel, $1/8$-in. (3mm) parting tool, $3/8$-in. (10mm) beading and parting tool.

A selection of scrapers used to refine a surface.

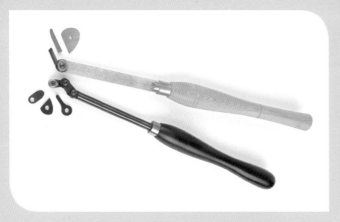

An alternative to standard-shaped scrapers is to opt for multi-tipped tools. Depending on the tips available, these can be used to hollow out work as well as for refining surfaces.

Tip Scrapers should be placed on the lathe rest and used in trailing mode, with the handle higher than the cutting edge so as to minimize the risk of a catch.

The second route, which is probably cheaper and more flexible, is to opt for a multi-tipped tool. This is effectively a handled bar onto which a variety of tips can be fitted. There are many types and makes available, including versions with round, square or shaped bars.

Most multi-tipped tools come as a package with a selection of tips, and they often either include a facility to swivel the tip or have an articulated head arrangement to alter the tip position. There are large tips for refining work in the same way as with conventional scrapers; and smaller tips to help with hollowing out work, particularly end grain. These can, of course, also be used on faceplate-grain work, and for deeper work. I drill some of the holes I require in cylinders, but tools like these are ideal for creating deep hollow areas.

If you use a version with a round bar, the tip can be presented in standard scraping mode or rotated so the cutter is in shear-scraping mode for a finer cut.

BEAD FORMING TOOLS

I use bead forming tools quite a lot. You can of course practice your turning skills and turn beads with a gouge, or a beading and parting tool, or similar, but you will find bead forming tools can solve various issues. They are, for example, very useful in hard to reach areas that are tricky to cut with conventional tools and also when needing lots of the same sized beads close together. I do use larger bead forming tools, but I favor small $1/8$-in. (3mm) or $3/16$-in. (5mm) ones to create well-detailed, delicate beads. Such tools are a luxury, of course, and you can get by with other ones, but these beads do require good tool control to get right.

Bead forming tools typically come in two types. One type has a flute milled down the length of the blade, or partially down the blade. These are used with the flute down on the rest, and the cutting edge is gently pushed into the wood until you get to the required bead form. The lower three tools in the picture are examples of this type. The wider forming tool on the top left-hand side is an example of the other type of bead forming tool which has a bead profile ground into the end of the blade. It is effectively a shaped scraper and as such is used in scraping mode, where the handle is either horizontal to the work or is held higher than the cutting tip in contact with the work.

Do not use either type of tool to reduce the diameter of the work; only use them on the surface of the wood. The crown of the bead should be the tip of the surface being worked to.

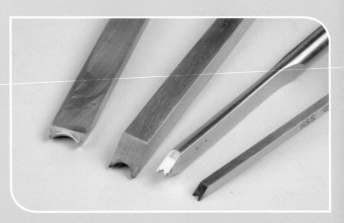

Bead forming tools.

ABRASIVES

After shaping your work, you will need to sand it to a fine finish. There are numerous grit grades and types of abrasive to choose from. I would recommend aluminum oxide to start with. It is up to you whether you use it by hand or use loop-backed abrasive attached to sanding arbors held in a drill.

I use both hand and power sanding methods. You should not power sand right up against details such as beads and coves. These areas should only be sanded by hand. If power sanding, a 2- or 3-in. (50 or 75mm) arbor is all that is needed for these projects. Of course, to power sand you will need a drill. You will also need one when drilling a hole for a screw chuck, and most people have one in their workshop.

The projects require nothing finer than 400 grit to finish. I have used 120, 180, 240, 320 and 400 grit abrasives. Of course, use coarser or finer if you need, but whatever grit grade you start with, it should be coarse enough to remove any damage or surface deviation. Then, use successively finer grit grades to remove the scratches left by the previous one, until you cannot see them any more. Always work through the grits, and never skip any.

Drum or round cylinder-type sanding arbors are also useful pieces of equipment. They clean up holes quickly and easily. The smaller ones can be used to create detail, too, as in the Money box project (see page 40).

Tip A pair of forceps is very useful when working on vases and hollow forms. I use them for holding abrasives and also cloth when sanding or finishing in hard to reach places. **Warning:** never hold forceps by the handle holes, only hold the shaft. If you ever get a catch with them, you do not want your fingers trapped in the holes.

One piece of sanding equipment that has been incredibly productive in making the turned toys for this book is a disc sander. An inverted belt sander will also work well. You will be able to work out how to finish off your turnings with the equipment you have, but over the years we usually acquire things that make life a little easier. These days, a disc sander is something that I would hate to be without.

Drill, abrasive, sanding accessories and power sanding arbors.

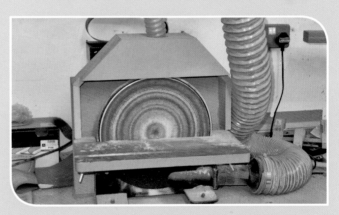

A disc sander with appropriate extraction.

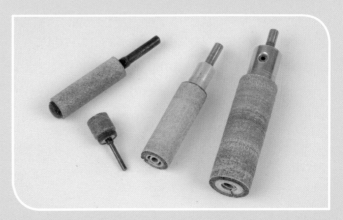

Drum sander and round sanding arbors for rotary handpieces or drills.

ADDITIONAL WORKSHOP SUPPLIES

There are a few other pieces of equipment used in this book that, although often overlooked, are nonetheless useful. When measuring and marking, you will need a rule, a tape measure, a depth gauge and calipers of some sort. We all need to know sizes and gauge things accurately for fit.

I use a screw chuck for some work, which requires a drill and a suitable drill bit. I also use a drill chuck with a Morse taper to suit the tailstock quill of the

lathe. Into a drill chuck can be fitted drill bits of various sizes, including large sawtooth or Forstner bits. These larger bits are a good alternative to hollowing tools. You can use hollowing tools if you wish, but if you can find large-sized bits at the right price they are often more accurate and easier to use.

If you need to drill holes with perfect accuracy on items that are not held on the lathe, a drill press comes in very useful. It should be used in conjunction with a vise, clamps or other holding device. For example, have a look at the rectangular undercarriage sections for the Train project (see page 94).

Buying pre-dimensioned wood can be expensive, and it is not always available in the sizes needed, so I make good use of a bandsaw. When you are working with odd-shaped parts, you are also likely to need jigs, clamps and hot-melt glue to support securely the work being cut. I often use clamps to hold work while it is being drilled, cut or glued. What type you use is up to you, but having different-sized clamps available is always helpful.

I like to use a rotary carving unit, into which can be fitted shaping and cutting burrs and discs. This is another of those items that is not essential but can make life much easier for woodworkers.

Handsaws and chisels are useful for cutting, adjusting and refining. I use a flush-cut saw quite a lot, and a few carving and bench chisels. It is always a question of selecting the right tool for the right task. In one project, I used a knife to make the necessary cuts.

I have one last piece of equipment that is worth mentioning, and that is a sphere-cutting jig. A couple of toys, such as the Penguin skittles (see page 66), need spheres cutting. I show you how to do this by hand, and using a jig. If you are making a lot of spheres, a dedicated jig will give you precision that hand cutting will not. Slight variances in hand turning might not make much difference, but if you need a lot of spheres at exactly the same size, or you need one made to exacting tolerances, a specialist jig can save no end of time and hassle.

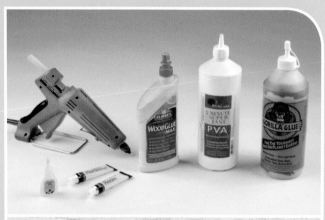

A range of adhesives gives you options as to what to use.

Adhesives

No workshop is complete without a range of adhesives. PVA, aliphatic resin and epoxy all have their place. However, be careful to make sure adhesive is non-toxic when dry and fully cured if it is being used on toys that might end up being put in a child's mouth. Safety considerations should always be kept in mind when creating turned toys (see page 12).

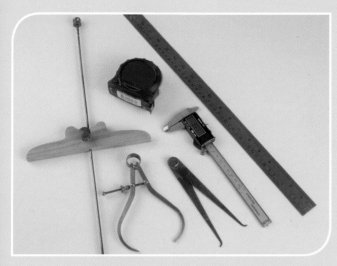

A variety of measuring and marking equipment is a must to ensure accuracy in what you are making.

A couple of carving tools and a pocket knife or carving knife will come in handy for some projects.

A drill, drill chuck and drill bits and cutters will help with projects.

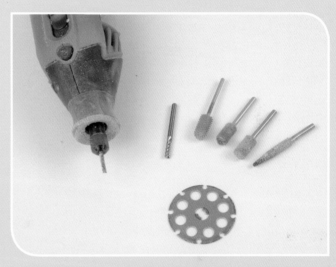

A rotary carving tool is a very handy piece of equipment. It will come in very useful on a few projects in the book, but it isn't essential.

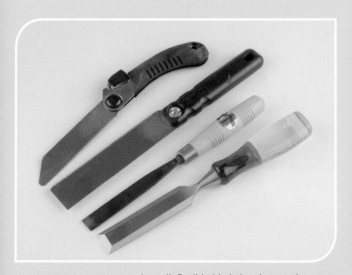

A small, flexible-blade handsaw and a gouge and chisel are useful tools to have.

For cutting multiple spheres of a specific size, a purpose-built jig will ensure accuracy. But you can hand-turn the spheres too.

Wood

When making toys, you need to use wood and other materials that will not splinter, crack or shatter easily, so that the toys are safe for children to play with. You should ensure that the wood or material you work with is suited to its intended use.

For this book, I have not taken the prescriptive 'what woods to use' approach. The reason for this is that availability of the various types of wood differs wildly from area to area, and from country to country. I have, however, made recommendations as to the type of wood that is suitable for the project. The norm is to use close-grained, dense woods when making toys, because these can be worked easily and hold details well. Typically, woods including maple and sycamore (*Acer* spp.), beech (*Fagus* spp.), birch (*Betula* spp.) and fruitwoods work well, but there are myriad woods that are suitable and have their own special qualities.

One project uses softwood, which can be either spruce (*Picea* spp.) or fir (*Abies* spp.). I also used a high-quality laminated birch-faced ply for some projects, which has many layers to it. Known also as Scandinavian multi-lam ply, it is supremely strong and dimensionally stable, and you can laminate up large sections that are both stable and cheaper than solid wood of the same size. Such ply is also wonderful to use where smaller, thinner items are required, where normal wood sections would crack across the grain. On the downside, this material can be very dusty to work, it blunts tools quickly, and occasionally there may be some voids in the laminations (although that is rare). Always cut ply carefully with sharp tools to avoid grain pull-out or tear-out.

There are many wonderful woods available, and the choices are endlessly fascinating. Whether you decide to make toys from woods that are local or

Selection of wood, ready for turning:
(A) maple, **(B)** oak, **(C)** sycamore, **(D)** cherry, **(E)** ash, **(F)** plywood, **(G)** birch, **(H)** poplar, **(I)** apple, **(J)** beech, **(K)** American cherry, **(L)** boxwood.

Ply laminated to resemble wood with grain orientated for bowl or faceplate work.

from far-flung locations is up to you, but do always use wood that comes from a sustainable source. Look for the FSC logo or double-check with your supplier to make sure that your wood has come from a well-managed forest or source.

Wood size is not specified for each project, as the items can be scaled up or down as you choose. You can, though, find the finished sizes and dimensions on the accompanying drawings. If you are following these, just select a piece of wood that is slightly larger than the sizes given.

In each project, I also state whether each wood section is a spindle- or end-grain orientated section, where the grain of the wood runs parallel to the lathe bed bars; or is a faceplate- or bowl-grain orientated section, where the wood grain runs at 90 degrees to the lathe bed bars.

Waste-wood chucks

In the projects, I show you how to do reverse turning, and how to hold wood between centers using friction drives made from offcuts of waste wood.

I keep all the offcuts in the workshop, as they can be used as cheap friction drives and jam chucks, as well as being altered to suit various jobs. They are a low-cost option to solving problems, and you will find many ingenious uses as you venture further into turning. One neat friction-drive method is used in the process of turning spheres for the Penguin skittles project (see page 66).

A selection of waste-wood friction drives and jam chucks.

Sphere held between two hollow-ended friction chucks/drives.

Ply laminated to resemble spindle- or end-grain orientated wood.

Health and safety

Woodturning poses some risks to the turner. There are sharp tools, spinning wood, and debris that flies from the work – often at very high speed, as the work is being shaped and cut. It is fundamental that you look after yourself and use some of the personal protective equipment (PPE) that is available to help minimize the dangers.

First and foremost, make sure that you protect your eyes and face. As a minimum, eye protection should be used. Better still, use a full-face shield to avoid the risk of damage from flying shavings and chippings.

You also need to protect yourself from dust. This is not only produced during the cutting stages, but also at the final sanding stages. Various types of mask and respirator-type filter systems fitted over the nose and mouth are available. These come in different shapes and sizes, and are rated for use in certain environments and with particular materials and chemicals. They can be disposable, or they can be permanent equipment with replaceable filters to ensure high performance every time they are used. Check that the ones you buy are suitable for the work you will be doing.

Recent developments have seen the cost of powered respirators fall. These have a battery-operated filtering system and also offer full-face protection. There are numerous types, but they all operate in a similar way. Again, check the rating of the filters to make sure that you have the right one for the job.

Although respirators protect you to some degree, chippings and dust still need to be removed from the working area. Large, vacuum-type systems, with an extraction point close to the work, will remove the bulk of the material produced and are the best way of dealing with dust and chippings. Finer, ambient air-filtration systems will remove smaller particles.

Tip When applying finishes, either with the lathe stationary or with the piece removed from the lathe, using protective gloves will reduce skin contact with potentially harmful finishes.

Personal protective equipment (PPE) is essential.

Operating a lathe safely

- Double-check that the work is held securely and everything is locked in place before switching on the lathe.

- Rotate the work by hand to ensure the rest is clear of the spinning work.

- Make sure that you are not wearing loose sleeves or items of clothing or jewelry that can get caught in the work. Tie long hair back out of the way.

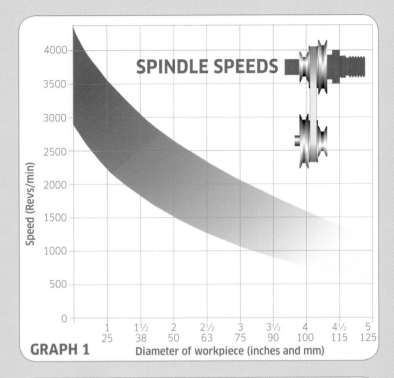

GRAPH 1

Speed (Revs/min) — SPINDLE SPEEDS

Diameter of workpiece (inches and mm)

| 1 | 1½ | 2 | 2½ | 3 | 3½ | 4 | 4½ | 5 |
| 25 | 38 | 50 | 63 | 75 | 90 | 100 | 115 | 125 |

LATHE SPEED

Setting the correct lathe speed is important. If you set it too high, you might end up with the wood flying off the lathe, vibrating too much, or even exploding if the wall is too thin or there is a flaw. I have included speed charts here that provide a handy reference for faceplate and spindle projects, based on the size of the work.

As a rule of thumb, the larger the work, the slower the safe working speed on the lathe will be. The fact that the charts specify a speed range is not enough in itself: common sense also comes into play. Recommended speeds are based on the assumption that the wood is perfectly sound, and that there are no flaws, splits, cracks, fissures, bark inclusions or unevenness (such as being square or out of balance).

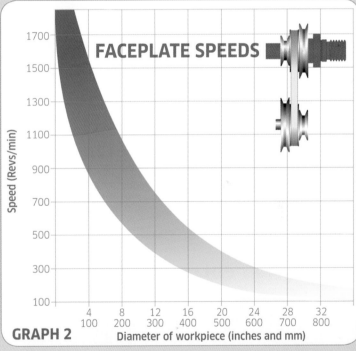

GRAPH 2

Speed (Revs/min) — FACEPLATE SPEEDS

Diameter of workpiece (inches and mm)

| 4 | 8 | 12 | 16 | 20 | 24 | 28 | 32 |
| 100 | 200 | 300 | 400 | 500 | 600 | 700 | 800 |

Let me say that no wood for toys should have any flaws in it, but it may be out of balance. The best advice is to work within the recommended parameters; but if in doubt at any time, stop the lathe, check the piece and assess if it is safe to continue. If it is, then proceed slowly.

Finishing and fixing

How you finish your toys is entirely up to you. I have chosen to color a lot of the projects in this book, but you can leave the wood in its natural state if you prefer. Make sure you use products that are safe and suitable for use on children's toys.

You can color your projects in exactly the same way as I have, or you can decide to use another type of finish. There are plenty of products about that are non-toxic. Look around for finishes that are clearly labeled as 'Safe for use on toys' or 'Toy safe'. This should be marked in writing and logos.

You have lots of finishes to choose from, including natural and brightly colored dyes, lacquers, waxes, oils and paint, and toy-safe pens. Do be aware that color is there to finish and highlight your work, not to cover over bad turning, torn grain or other defects. Your surface preparation and sanding must be thorough to achieve the best results.

Cloths, paper towels, brushes and cleaning materials are all useful in the finishing of work. Just find the implements and materials that you like, and which are suitable for the project, and go for it. This is the ideal moment to get children to help. They love this part of the making process.

FIXINGS AND PULL-APART JOINTS

Some toys benefit from having parts that lock together. In the Tea party, some of the cakes have joints than can be pulled apart by hand, or separated with a toy knife (see page 160). The Pull–along train (see page 94) uses a magnet-and-bolt arrangement to link the engine to the carriages so that they can be pulled along.

One option for joints is a spigot and recess. It is not the most aesthetically pleasing, but it is useful for items such as muffins and cupcakes. You can also

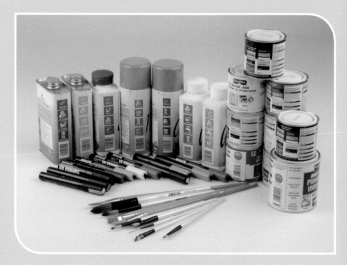

Lacquers, wax, oil, paints, brushes and pens.

Concentrated dyes.

Oils and waxes.

use discs of hook-and-loop fixings (such as Velcro). These need to be glued in place, with a small recess cut in the surface of the work just shallower than the depth of the disc being fitted. The hook-and-loop fixing then sits just proud of the surface, and attaches very nicely to a corresponding disc.

Magnets are an interesting option, and their use is increasingly popular. Various types can be used, but I have chose rare earth magnets, which are small and unobtrusive. You simply mark the correct alignment positions, drill a hole of suitable width and depth, and glue in place. Before gluing, make sure the polarities are correct, so that corresponding magnets lock together and don't push apart.

When using hook-and-loop fixings or magnets, you need to be careful that your adhesive fixes everything in place properly so that it has no way of coming loose. The small parts represent a choke hazard, and magnets are not a good thing to be swallowing. Epoxy resin adhesive works well for me when I want a secure fixing. As mentioned before, lock everything in place and, if in any doubt about its security, find an alternative method to do the job.

There are many more fixing options than I have used in the book, but I have tried to employ those that are most suitable and easily achievable.

A safety reminder

Make sure that what you are making is age appropriate, with suitable size, weight and construction method.

• Be aware of potential problem areas when making toys, and make sure you design things to deal with these issues. Consider splinters, small parts, breakage risks, sharp points and toxic finishes.

• If in any doubt whatsoever, don't do it! Change the process or design to solve the problem.

• Be safe when turning. Don't forget to work as safely as you can at all times.

• Remember to get the children involved in the work at a safe and suitable stage.

A spigot and recess was used to connect this cupcake.

Hook-and-loop fixings are good for a joint that can be repeatedly separated.

Magnets were used to connect a pork pie.

Traditional Toys
and **Games**

Children love toy animals, and turning them is always an enjoyable challenge. I wanted to make a one-piece project, and started looking at examples of toys that might not require joints. I discovered some wonderful little hedgehogs turned by my friend Lesley Churton. With Lesley's blessing, and inspired by her animals, I created my own hedgehogs.

Hedgehogs

Tools and materials

PPE: facemask/respirator

Drive spur and revolving center

Chuck

Spindle roughing gouge

Spindle gouge

Skew chisel

Abrasives, 120–400 grit

Thin parting tool

Saw

Finishing oil

Paints, toy-safe pens or pyrography machine

I didn't know the exact process Lesley used, until after making these hedgehogs and a few others. It is always nice to have a starting point and then experiment, ending up with different takes on a theme.

These hedgehogs are created from end-grain, or spindle-grain, oriented wood. They use simple offset techniques, also known as eccentric or multi-axis turning. Such turning is exciting, but having a non-centralized piece running on a lathe scares some people. With a few guidelines, there really is nothing to worry about.

I decided to use two offset turning positions, as a gentle introduction to offset turning. You can use more off-center positions and more radical offsets, and experimentation is the key to success. I used brown oak (*Quercus* sp.) for my hedgehogs, but ash (*Fraxinus* spp.), maple (*Acer* spp.), walnut (*Juglans* spp.) and fruitwoods will all work beautifully, too.

Lesley's hedgehogs, the inspiration for this project.

TOP VIEW

Note that metric conversions have been
rounded up. Use either imperial or metric
measurements, and do not mix the two.

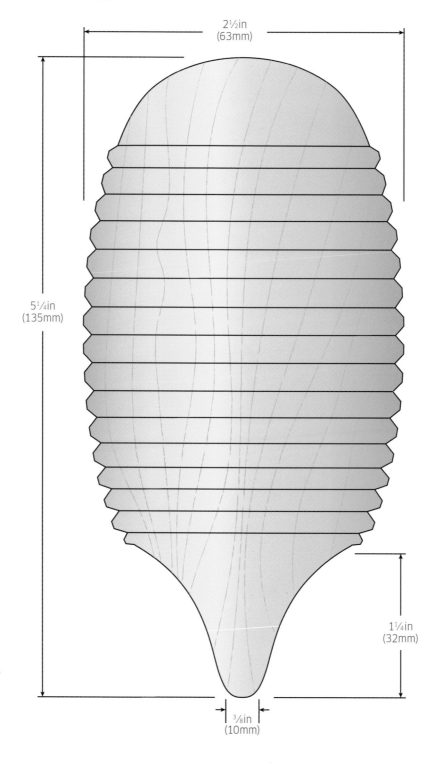

2½in
(63mm)

5¼in
(135mm)

1¼in
(32mm)

³⁄₈in
(10mm)

1 For offset turning, you need to make sure that there is as good a hold on the wood as possible. I used a revolving ring center and a toothed Steb drive center for this, as this combination works well on dry wood. However, a standard two- or four-prong drive and point revolving center will work too.

2 Mark the central line on both ends of the wood (the horizontal line shown here), 1³/₄ in. (45mm) in from one side. On what will be the head of the hedgehog (the tailstock end when mounted between centers), draw the lower line (A) so that it strikes across the central line 1 in. (25mm) up from the bottom edge. On both ends of the wood, draw the second line (B) 1¹/₄ in. (32mm) up from the bottom edge.

3 Now mount the wood between centers on the (B) positions.

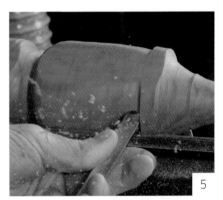

4 Use a spindle roughing gouge to turn the wood so that you have three-quarters of the wood rounded, leaving a flat bottom.

5 With the spindle gouge, block in the shape. Create a sloping nose, and shape the body to suggest the form of a hedgehog.

Safety warning

Because the wood is mounted eccentrically on the lathe, make sure that your lathe speeds are set slower than if the wood were mounted concentrically. Also check the rest position and move the wood by hand to ensure it clears the tool rest before restarting the lathe.

6 Note the flat on the bottom. You can turn this piece straight between centers and sand off a flat bottom if you like, but the technique we are using is more fun. The back end of the hedgehog is partially shaped, but enough thickness is left to support the piece when off-aligned later. The tailstock end is still quite wide, so the center will fit wholly at point A later on.

7 Once you have the overall form shaped, reposition your revolving center on point A.

8 Working only on the head end, use a spindle gouge to create a tighter, flatter face. Blend it into the nose end, but be careful not to make the tip of the nose too narrow at this stage. Otherwise, you will be unable to reposition the revolving center on point B. Once you have the shape you want, remount the revolving center on point B.

9 Use the spindle gouge to remove more waste in the area of the hedgehog's bottom, leaving about 1¼ in. (32mm) of thickness to make sure of stability. Clean up the rest of the waste to create a spigot to fit your chuck.

10 To represent the spines on the hedgehog, I cut grooves with the point of a skew chisel held in horizontal scraping mode. This technique minimizes the risk of catches if you are unfamiliar with using a skew chisel. That said, the finish in the grooves is not quite as good as when you cut them conventionally using the slicing cut, working from either side to create the groove.

11 Once the grooves are cut, sand all the available areas to a fine finish. Don't round the grooves over too far, just soften the edges slightly so that there are no splinters.

12 You should now have a nicely shaped hedgehog.

13 With delicate cuts of the spindle gouge, refine the shape of the snout, but stop short of the revolving center.

14 Sand the snout area.

15 Remove the hedgehog from the lathe, and mount it in the chuck on the spigot that you formed in step 9.

16 When the piece is secure, and with the lathe switched off, saw off the end of the snout.

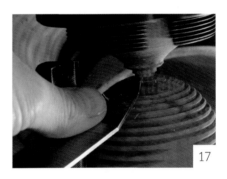

17 Use a thin parting tool to cut part of the way through the waste at the headstock end, before stopping the lathe and sawing it off. Once off the lathe, sand this end round and smooth.

Tip You can make bigger and smaller hedgehogs, and vary their shapes, materials and the expressions on their faces. Experiment until you have created a whole family of these irresistible wooden creatures.

18 Use paints, toy-safe pens or a pyrography machine to add the eyes. I finished this hedgehog with finishing oil.

This is a simple puzzle that gets people thinking. The objective is to remove the central, pointed cylinder from the inside of its holder without touching any part of the two pieces. It is a two-part project that uses spindle-grain oriented wood, and the key to getting everything to work is mastering the shapes and tolerances.

Wooden puzzle

Tools and materials

PPE: facemask/respirator

Drive spur and revolving center

Chuck

Spindle roughing gouge

Spindle gouge

Beading and parting tool

Skew chisel

Abrasives, 120–400 grit

Wax

Thin parting tool

Paper towel

I used an exotic wood called cocobolo (*Dalbergia retusa*), obtained from a properly managed and licensed source, for the outside of this puzzle, while the inside is turned from European sycamore (*Acer pseudoplatanus*), a member of the maple family. This gave me a high color contrast without having to color the wood. You could use walnut or a similar dark wood to achieve the contrast. You could also use a wood such as sycamore throughout, then color one of the two pieces to add contrast.

The result of your turning is a tricky puzzle to solve. You are not allowed to tip the table over or slide the piece off the table by tilting it! Even if you hold the container, the taper of the cone is such that you won't be able to grip it. Also, the lower edge of the cone shape is below the surface of the container in which it sits, providing another obstacle to lifting it out. The solution to the puzzle is revealed at the end of the project.

Safety warning

The small parts represent a choking hazard for children under three years of age, so if you make the puzzle for children, it should be for those who are older than that age group.

CONTAINER PROFILE

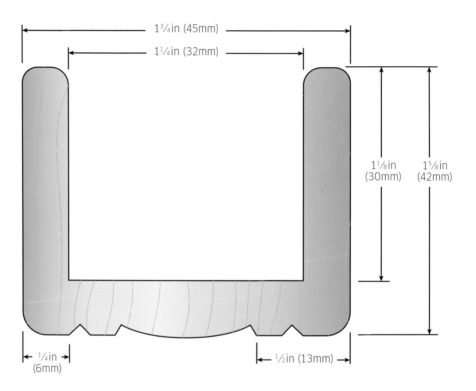

1¾in (45mm)

1¼in (32mm)

1⅛in (30mm)

1⅝in (42mm)

¼in (6mm)

½in (13mm)

CYLINDER SIDE VIEW

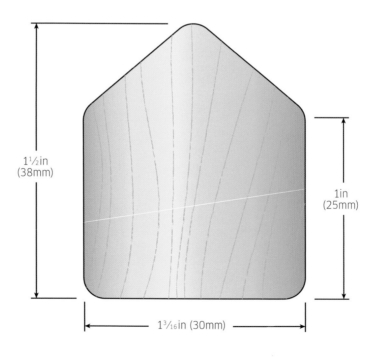

1½in (38mm)

1in (25mm)

1³⁄₁₆in (30mm)

1 Start by making the container. Mount your wood between centers or, as I did, fit it in the internal sections of the jaws. Using a spindle roughing gouge, turn a cylinder of the right diameter, to a length just longer than you need. The piece of wood used here was longer than required, but the offcut was not wasted as it could be used as a decorative insert for a box lid.

2 Hollow the inside with a spindle gouge. Start by setting the rest so that the gouge can be presented horizontally, with the tip aligned dead on center and the flute at the 10 o'clock position. Then, with the lathe running, push the blade in to about 3/8 in. (10mm) before extracting it.

3 Presenting the gouge in the same way, push it into the wood about 1/4 in. (6mm) and pull the gouge across the work. Cut on the lower wing as you go, stopping just shy of the required internal dimension.

4 Repeat stages 2 and 3 until you have almost reached the required internal depth.

5 Use a beading and parting tool to clean up the bottom of the hole to the required depth. The thickness of the blade will cause the top of the blade to hit the upper arc of the cylinder, so you cannot clean up the side wall with this tool.

6 To clean up the side wall, use a skew chisel, laying it on its side in scraping mode, with the long, pointed edge up against the side wall area. Be careful to create a nice clean intersection between the side wall and the bottom – there should be no deep grooves at this point.

7 Note that there is a small raised bit in the middle that I missed. I used the beading and parting tool to clean this up prior to sanding the inside. Instead of hollowing the inside by turning, you could drill it out and then clean up the bottom to remove the indent.

8 Use a gouge or the skew chisel in scraping mode to radius the inside and outside top edges. Then, sand all accessible areas to a very fine grit grade. Apply a coat of wax inside and out. Once the wax is applied, measure and part off the piece at the required depth with a thin parting tool.

9 You now have two options. One is just to sand the bottom and wax it. The other is to add some detail. If you opt to do this, you need to create a jam chuck to hold the piece so that you can access the bottom section. For this, a spigot of the right size for the internal hole needs to be created.

10 Make sure you test for fit (this image shows that adjustment is required). The shoulders of the container need to hit the rear vertical wall of the jam chuck. It needs to be tight but not too tight – just sufficiently snug to hold the piece.

11 Lay paper towel over the spigot and slide on the container section, creating an even tighter fit. Paper towel protects the inside while you add a detail, such as the button I chose. Do check the hold before turning on the lathe.

12 If you have followed the route of using a jam chuck – I used sycamore for mine – this piece can be used to create the internal pointed cylinder. I used the beading and parting tool to extend the cylinder length. If you didn't use a jam chuck, you can create this piece from a different cylinder of wood.

13 Keep checking the fit as you go along, as it needs to be snug. The internal cylinder needs to be longer than the inside of the container so that the pointed section can be created.

14 Extend the cylinder's length to the point where you can start cutting the cone-shaped head section where the lower edge sits just below the radiused top of the container. Use the spindle gouge to start to create the cone profile. Don't make it too thin at the pointed end at this stage.

15 Once you have the length of the parallel section defined, use the spindle gouge to clean up the bottom so that it is square across. Adjust the diameter of the cylinder so that you have a clearance gap of $1/64$ in. (0.5mm) all the way round between the central cylinder and the side wall of the container. Sand all accessible surfaces.

The solution

Blow hard across the piece to create a vacuum which causes the middle section to come out. You could pour in water to displace the middle section. This works, but it is messy and not what was intended!

16 Refine the cone-shaped top. It should not be too pointy, nor too blunt. You can use the skew chisel to make the final cut and part it off, but you risk getting grain tear-out at the point.

17 Note the grain tear-out. After this happened, I wrapped the piece in paper towel and held it gently in the central section of the chuck jaws while I cleaned it off. No finish was applied to the sycamore. Fit the two pieces together.

There are many ways to create money boxes, and they come in all shapes and sizes. I made one out of sycamore (*Acer pseudoplatanus*), in the style of an old-fashioned pillar box. This is a spindle-grain project and is really nothing more elaborate than an extra-tall box with the addition of a slot to place money in.

Money box

In this project I have kept things simple and just placed a removable lid on the box, which needs to be a tight fit. However, if you wish, you can add numerous anti-opening devices to stop someone dipping in before the money box is full.

For example, you could drill a hole and insert a rod in a strategic place on the join area. When painted, this will create a secret lock and only you will know its position, ensuring the money is safe until it's time for the owner of the box to cash in their savings.

Tools and materials

PPE: facemask/respirator

Chuck, drive spur and revolving center

Beading and parting tool

Bead forming tool

Spindle gouge

Thin parting tool

Handsaw

Sawtooth bit, 2⅜ in. (60mm)

Drill chuck and Morse taper

Round nose, French curve or shear scraper

Side-cut scraper or skew chisel

Abrasives, 120–400 grit

Rotary carving tool with drum sander, ⅜–½ in. (10–13mm)

Forceps or rod with hook-faced ball

Loop-backed abrasive

Spindle roughing gouge

Rotary carving tool, straight cutting bit

File

Primer and gloss paint

Cordless drill and sanding arbor

⅛–¼ in. (3–6mm) parallel cutter to cut a slot

Extended reach sanding unit

Paper towel

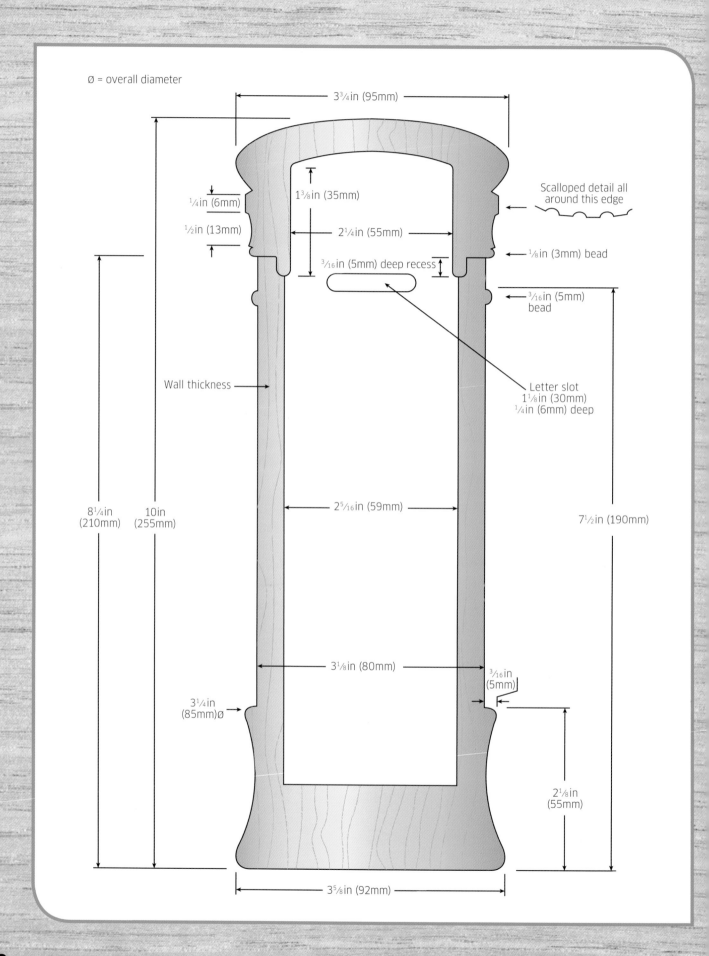

Ø = overall diameter

3³⁄₄in (95mm)

¹⁄₄in (6mm)

1³⁄₈in (35mm)

¹⁄₂in (13mm)

2¹⁄₄in (55mm)

³⁄₁₆in (5mm) deep recess

Scalloped detail all around this edge

¹⁄₈in (3mm) bead

³⁄₁₆in (5mm) bead

Wall thickness

Letter slot
1¹⁄₈in (30mm)
¹⁄₄in (6mm) deep

8¹⁄₄in (210mm)

10in (255mm)

2⁵⁄₁₆in (59mm)

7¹⁄₂in (190mm)

3¹⁄₈in (80mm)

³⁄₁₆in (5mm)

3¹⁄₄in (85mm)Ø

2¹⁄₈in (55mm)

3⁵⁄₈in (92mm)

1 Create a cylinder between centers and then mount it in your chuck. Keeping the tailstock in place for support, use a beading and parting tool to cut a spigot at the tailstock end. This end will become the lid, which you can now start shaping. The top should have a dome form.

2 The lower section of the lid should have a hollow shape like half a cove. When you are happy with the depth of the lid, use the beading and parting tool, a bead forming tool or a spindle gouge to cut a bead on the outer bottom edge. This will be the mating joint with the base. Also cut a shoulder fillet, which is the area that will have the scalloped detail on it later. This should be done just below the main dome of the lid.

3 Use the gouge to refine the rolled-over edge of the lid above the fillet. Refine the middle hollow and create a raised lip – almost a bead – above the spigot that will be the section that locks into the lower part of the pillar box. You can use the bead forming tool for this, or a gouge.

4 Use the thin parting tool to part almost all the way through, then stop the lathe. Remove the tailstock and saw through the remaining middle bit to free the lid.

5 Now it is time to hollow out the inside. On shallower projects, you can use conventional turning tools to create a hollow. However, as you go deeper and create more of an overhang over the rest of the tool, the more you require a thicker section of tool to minimize flexing and vibration. With a restricted opening like this one, tool presentation becomes difficult, so you end up scraping at the very end or having to use specialist hollowing rigs to hold and stabilize the tools. At this depth, drilling makes sense and is so much easier. I used a sawtooth bit held in a drill chuck, held in turn in the tailstock quill via a Morse taper.

6 Remove the bit regularly to get rid of shavings and dust and do not use the extraction in case any hot bits get taken into the collection bags. Ambient extraction is close by, but you can see the dust, smoke and steam. The wood in the center is not as dry as the outer section, hence the steam.

7 It is worth measuring and marking the depth of the hole to see where you are and where you need to drill to.

8 Once drilled to the desired depth, return the base section to the chuck and hollow out the inside. I started by using the spindle gouge with the flute well over, working from the center out to the spigot section, leaving the wall thickness of the spigot at about ³⁄₈ in. (10mm).

9 Use a conventional round-nose or French curve scraper to create a hollow to mimic the top dome; or use a shear scraper tilted at an angle to create a fine shearing cut, to minimize torn grain. Remember, work from the middle out to the outer area.

10 Use a side-cut scraper, or a skew on its side, to refine the side wall, creating a nice intersection between the hollow and the parallel side wall. Then sand the inside.

11 Now it is time to create the small detail on the fillet under the lip of the top of the pillar box. A rotary carving tool fitted with a drum sander will enable you to cut the small cove-like details. You can use an indexing unit and mark these precisely, but I did them by eye. The abrasive sleeve sat just beyond the front end, so I could get very close to the rounded lip without the top screw of the drum sander touching and marking the work.

12

13

14

12 Use the corner of a skew to clean up the top of the cut detail by creating a V-like chamfer top and bottom. I also cut a small V above the lower bead near the spigot, to create a nice detail. Slightly undercutting the lower face of the bead next to the spigot helps it seat perfectly against the base unit. Now, remove the piece from the chuck.

13 Remount the base and use the skew to create the female mating recess to accept the spigot on the lid. This needs to be a tight fit, so check regularly to see if it is the correct size.

14 Use the gouge or beading and parting tool to reduce the main body to the required diameter. It should be slimmer than the lower bead section of the top, but not so thin as to make the money box fragile.

15

16

17

15 Check the lid again for fit, and adjust the recess as necessary to ensure a snug fit. Note how the main body is slimmer than the lower bead.

16 You need to create a bead lower down the main body to act as a boundary for what is effectively a plain band, for the money slot, between this and the lower bead of the lid. Use the gouge, parting tool or, as shown here, the bead forming tool. It is the same bead size as the one cut earlier with a gouge.

17 Sand the inside. For this you can use an extension unit in a drill that accepts a sanding arbor; forceps to hold the abrasive; or, as shown here, a rod with a hook-faced ball on the end to which loop-backed abrasive is fitted.

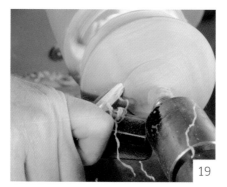

18 Remove and refit the lid, inserting paper towel between the lid and the base to ensure a secure hold that won't split the lid. Bring up the tailstock.

19 Use the spindle gouge to refine the dome on the top. As always, stop regularly and check the shape. Multiple light cuts will make life easy and enable you to adjust the shape without taking too much off.

20 When you are happy with the dome, remove the tailstock and turn away the remaining nub. Sand the top.

21 Use a spindle roughing gouge to remove some of the waste on the main section.

22 Cut a new bead, the same size as the upper one, lower down, to start to create the lower base section. This should be like an elongated cove, with a very fat, bead-like form at the bottom. The lower bead is the transition from the main parallel body to the base. I used the beading and parting tool to clean up just above this bead, and below the top one, to create the desired body width. With these two marks to work to, use any gouge you like to get the body even.

23 I didn't like the depth of the base section, so I elongated it using the spindle gouge. Don't ever be afraid to adjust something as you go. I had the thickness and length of wood available to do this, and the amendment created a better balance for the pillar box.

24 When you are happy with the base shape, sand the piece. Then, partially part through at the bottom section of the base, and saw off the piece.

25 Draw in the position of the letter slot. Be careful with the placement of the slot. It needs to be below where the spigot of the lid will eventually sit.

26 Now cut the slot. I used a rotary carving tool fitted with a straight cutting bit which has teeth on the end and side. This allows me to push and cut as required, being careful not to break out on the inside or deviate off the marked position. You can drill this slot before hollowing out, too, and then sand the shape after hollowing.

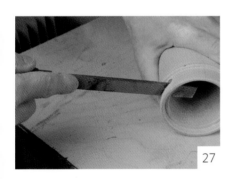

27 Using a file, or board with abrasive wrapped around it, sand the profile to the finished shape.

28 Now color the piece. I primed it, then left the primer to dry fully. I then used black gloss for the lower plinth, and left it to dry. Finally, I painted the main body and lid with a suitably bright red gloss.

If all goes to plan, you will end up with something like this striking pillar box-style money box. It should have a nice tight fit to the lid, which will come off only with a little persuasion.

I remember fondly playing with a whole box of different-shaped blocks in my childhood, building lovely things and, of course, knocking them down afterwards. Carefully made and beautifully colored, stacking blocks can be attractive pieces as well as making great toys.

Lighthouse stacker

Tools and materials

PPE: facemask/respirator

Drive spur and revolving center

Chuck

Drill chuck

Drill bit, 1⅜ in. (35mm)

Abrasives, 120–400 grit

Calipers

Bowl gouge

Spindle roughing gouge

Spindle gouge

Skew chisel

Beading and parting tool

Thin parting tool

Cordless drill and sanding arbor

Glue

Hammer

Toy-safe paints

Toy-safe pens

There are many variants of stacking blocks. The ones I had as a child were the 'freestyle' blocks, which you used to build whatever came into your head. Others, like the blocks in this project, are designed to represent something specific. Here, stacking blocks that graduate in size are assembled in the correct sequence to create a towering lighthouse.

Lighthouses, with their remote coastal locations and association with shipwrecks and rescues, are designed to capture the imagination. There is one near where I work, and it is a wonderfully iconic building whose tapering white-and-red ring structure works perfectly in the form of stacking blocks.

I must admit that I have made this lighthouse a little bit tricky for the person playing with it, and the child has to work out how to hold the blocks effectively. You could shape each graduated block as a doughnut shape – this is an easy shape to grip – but you could also create some deep V cuts on each intersection to provide another type of handhold. I also made the blocks quite heavy. Of course you can scale the lighthouse up or down, but if the blocks are too heavy and one is released by a child while they still have fingers under the block, there might be a nip/crush problem. Always be aware of the weight when making things – in this project, you could hollow out the underside of the blocks to lessen the weight.

To construct my wooden stacking-block lighthouse, I used high-quality, laminated birch-faced ply in combination with solid maple. I then added some decorative tricks to make it a convincing model.

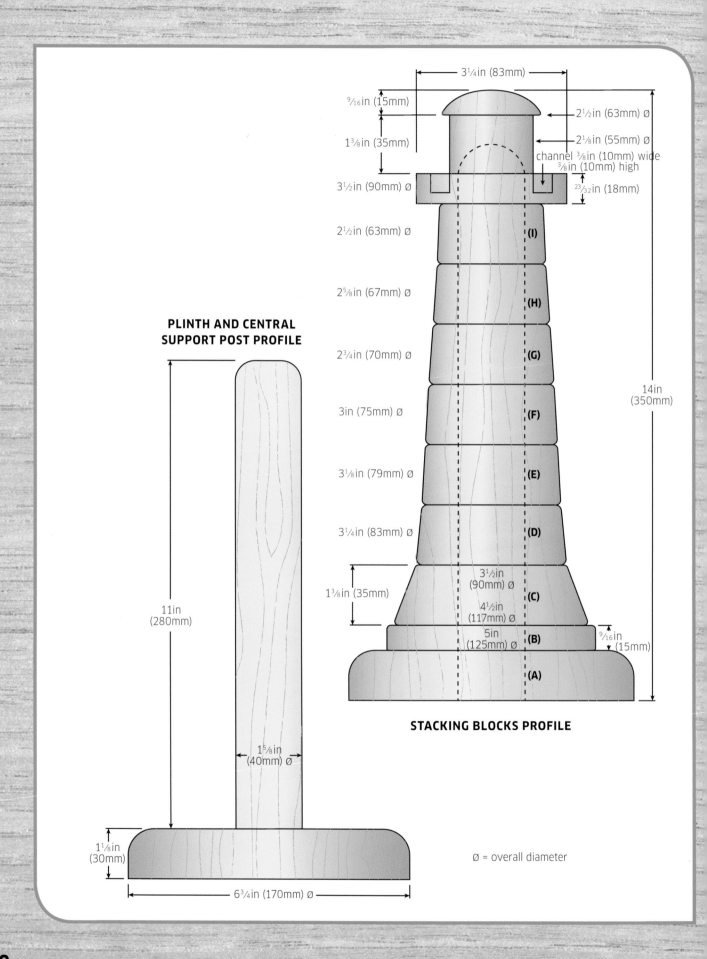

PLINTH AND CENTRAL SUPPORT POST PROFILE

11in (280mm)

1⅝in (40mm) Ø

1⅛in (30mm)

6¾in (170mm) Ø

3¼in (83mm)

⁹⁄₁₆in (15mm)

1⅜in (35mm)

3½in (90mm) Ø

2½in (63mm) Ø

2⅝in (67mm) Ø

2¾in (70mm) Ø

3in (75mm) Ø

3⅛in (79mm) Ø

3¼in (83mm) Ø

1⅜in (35mm)

3½in (90mm) Ø

4½in (117mm) Ø

5in (125mm) Ø

2½in (63mm) Ø

2⅛in (55mm) Ø

channel ⅜in (10mm) wide
⅜in (10mm) high

²³⁄₃₂in (18mm)

14in (350mm)

⁹⁄₁₆in (15mm)

(I)
(H)
(G)
(F)
(E)
(D)
(C)
(B)
(A)

STACKING BLOCKS PROFILE

Ø = overall diameter

1

2

1 I started off with a laminated ply block suitable for the bottom three parts (A, B, C). Mount this block between centers, true it up with a bowl gouge, and cut a recess in the lower section. At this point, remove the block from the lathe and mount it in the chuck. Now the block can be shaped. The lowest and widest of the three parts will form the base (A), into which you will later fit a central support post for the stacking blocks to slide down.

2 The diameter of the central support post is 1³/₈ in. (35mm), and a hole needs to be drilled or turned to accommodate it. I chose to drill with the appropriately sized bit held in a drill chuck in the headstock. While this requires more expensive kit, it is simpler and removes the need to measure everything again and again. Eventually the hole will be bored all the way through the laminate block, but at this stage it need only be deep enough to clear the first parting cut.

3

4

3 Once the piece is drilled, check you are happy with the shape. The top part of the block, which you are going to part off later with a thin parting tool, will form the lowest white band (C) of the lighthouse itself. It should have a wide base section and a gentle upward curve. Don't make this too steep, as the curve will run all the way to the top of the lighthouse and you don't want the top section so narrow that there is not enough wall thickness to fit on the central support post. Sand the top face and inner edge. Also, lightly sand inside the hole.

4 Clean up the face of the next part (B). This is a narrow ring that will form the black plinth on which the lighthouse stands. Drill the central hole so that it is deeper than the next parting cut. Sand the accessible parts. The edge of this disc should be square with a slight chamfer top and bottom.

5

6

5 When you are happy with the shape, part this piece off with a thin parting tool, remembering to remove the blade every so often to clear the cut of shavings and suchlike to prevent the blade from binding in the cut.

6 Now shape the remaining part, which will become the base (A). This should have a rounded outer edge profile, which is tactile and easy to hold. The shaping can be done with either a bowl or spindle gouge. Complete the drilling of the central hole that you began in step 2. The chuck jaws themselves have expanded well past the 1³/₈-in. (35mm) hole, so the drill cannot catch there. Between the ply block and the bottom of the chuck jaws, there is a 1-in. (25mm) gap. You can keep the piece on the lathe, slowly and gently moving the drill forward to cut just through but to stay clear of any metal parts. Alternatively, remove the piece and drill it off the lathe. Once it is drilled, sand all visible and safely accessible parts.

7

8

7 Create a waste-wood jam chuck that will lock into the hole drilled in the base. The spigot needs to be a tight enough fit to hold the base while you refine the recess underneath.

8 When you have created your jam chuck, mount the base on it with the underside outermost. Use a bowl or spindle gouge to clean up the underside, putting a chamfer on the recess section. Leave a ¹/₈-in. (3mm) dovetail or parallel side-wall section to lock in the chuck jaws later on. A parting tool can be used for this. Once shaped, sand to a smooth finish.

9 Next, create the central support post. I used a piece of maple (*Acer* sp.) for this. Mount between centers and roughly shape into a cylinder just over the 1³/₈-in. (35mm) diameter required. I used calipers and a beading and parting tool to achieve the correct measurement of 1³/₈ in. (35mm) at one end. This end will slot directly into the base, so it needs to be a good, tight fit.

10 Remove the post from the lathe and test for fit in the base section.

Tip Remember your speed graphs (see page 23): select the appropriate one for the size and condition of the piece you are working on. If in doubt, slow things down.

11 Remount the central support post between centers. Take down to 1³/₈ in. (35mm) with the spindle roughing gouge.

12 Cut a slot in the end of the central support post that fits into the base. Glue the post into the base, and fit a wedge in the slot to hold it all tightly in place. Don't worry about the excess part of the wedge at this point.

13

14

13 Remount the assembled piece on the lathe. Bringing up the tailstock will tell if everything is nicely centralized. I achieved this accurately by leaving a slight shoulder between the 1³/₈-in. (35mm) tenon created at the end of the central support post and the majority of the post turned at 1¹/₂ in. (38mm). When you are happy with the fit, remove from the lathe and set aside to dry. When dry, cut off the excess of the wedge and sand that area. Remount it, and turn the central support post down to 1³/₈ in. (35mm). Give it a good sand, so that the finished diameter is just smaller than 1³/₈ in. (35mm). Then round off the end of the support column with the gouge.

14 Now for the rest of the lighthouse. I chose to use laminated ply again, because it is dimensionally stable so should work well with no movement. The downside is the potential grain tear-out. Extra sanding, to avoid splinters, and an extra coat of undercoat should sort this out – well, it has so far for me. Mount the laminates to run lengthways on the spindle, like standard spindle-grain oriented wood. Turn a cylinder and form a spigot at one end to fit your chuck. Mount the piece in the chuck and drill a 1³/₈-in. (35mm) hole to a comfortable depth: it must be deep enough to clear the next parting cut.

15

16

15 Bring up a revolving center with a large enough head to fit and support the ply column in the hole drilled. Start shaping the rest of the lighthouse column. I used the bowl gouge for this. Remember, it should form a gentle, upsweeping curve. The tailstock end is the widest part now required, and the bottom of this part (D) should be the same diameter as the top of the lowest part of the lighthouse (C) cut in step 3.

16 Stop short of the headstock end, which will be the top of the lighthouse. Prior to parting off, release the tailstock end and sand the inside and visible face. Then, measure the appropriate depth of the next required block, and part off this section. Note how the tailstock is in place while the initial parting cut is made. It is released to cut off the ring.

17 Repeat this phase for the rest of the lighthouse column (blocks E to I). Drill or turn the central hole deeper each time as you progress to the next block section. I almost forgot to sand this piece, so stopped the lathe and sanded it prior to cutting all the way through.

18 Keep working along the cylinder. When drilling, remember to remove the cutter often enough to remove debris and to make sure the cutter remains sharp. Otherwise, you can end up with burning – see the smoke here?

19 Note how the combination of a blunt bit, perhaps too high a speed of lathe rotation, and the bit not moving fast enough into the wood resulted in the inside being charred. A bit of sanding will remove this, but it should not happen in the first place. This is the last piece of the main column before we create the top of the lighthouse.

20 Now to create the top three parts of the lighthouse. The remaining piece of ply was deliberately left wider for this purpose. You need to create a collar, which represents a walking gallery; a faux glass area for the light; and, finally, a cap. You can drill or turn the central hole – it needs to be just deep enough to sit on the support column, but not too deep. Once cut, clean up the end and reduce the outer diameter to that required.

21 Stop the lathe, load up all the sections and check for fit. Everything needs to push together. You will need to sand the meeting faces of all the blocks. This is easily done with abrasive on a table or on a sanding disc, to ensure everything fits together properly.

22 To get the shape and form right, remove the pieces from the lathe and remount the base section with the support column in the chuck. Load up all the blocks and what will be the top of the lighthouse. Adjust the shape with the bowl gouge.

23 Once the lighthouse body shape is correct, use the corner of a skew in scraping mode to create a V-cut between every join. This will help with the look, and when painted the joins will look like real building block sections.

24 Use a combination of gouge, beading and parting tool, and thin parting tool to shape the top section.

25 You can see how the thin parting tool is used to make a plunge cut, creating the depth of the walking gallery area.

26 The faux glass area for the light is shaped with the gouge. You can see this area and the gallery clearly defined, while the top has a nice dome. The outer edge of this should be wider than the faux glass section. When you have finished shaping, sand the whole piece thoroughly until it is smooth and all parts look good and seat properly.

27 Use the thin parting tool to almost cut through the last remaining stub of ply near the tailstock. Stop the lathe and remove the lighthouse. Carve off the last stub of ply, and sand smooth. The final job is to prime and undercoat the whole piece, using two coats of undercoat before applying the gloss. I used red and white gloss for the main lighthouse; a silver pen to color the light; and a white pen to create the diamonds of the glass. The base, plinth and gallery area were coated with black gloss.

Spinning tops have been treasured toys for many generations of children. Over the years there have been all sorts of designs and styles, and this offers the turner a chance to experiment with shape, proportions and tool control. Coloring your spinning tops – or, better still, letting your children or friends personalize their own – can be almost as much fun as turning and spinning them!

Spinning top

Tools and materials

PPE: facemask/respirator

Chuck, drive spur and revolving center

Spindle roughing gouge

Spindle gouge

Skew chisel

Abrasives, 120–400 grit

Drill press and clamp

5/8-in. (15mm) sawtooth drill bit

Disc sander

Hand-held rotary carving tool with 1/2-in. (13mm) drum sander

Wire

Toy-safe pens

Beading and parting tool

Thin parting tool

Cordless drill and 1/8-in. (3mm) drill bit

Cord

Gloss lacquer

Disc or belt

I have chosen to show you how to make a variant of the traditional 'whip' spinning top. This is a great project to teach children manual dexterity and hand-eye coordination. It is a spindle-turning project of three parts, and each part has the grain running parallel to the bed bars. You can make large or small versions to suit your space and needs; I made quite a large one, for use on a floor or patio.

Traditionally, you would have had a handle with a length of string or cord attached, which in turn was wound round the main body of the top. To spin the top, you held the handle and top – usually in one hand – and then threw the top at the same time as whipping the handle away in the opposite direction. This gave the top its spinning momentum before it landed on the ground.

My version has a handle that you slide onto the main shaft of the top. There is a separate cord, with a toggle handle, which is threaded into the main shaft and wound round it. Placing the spinning top on the floor, with only the balancing point touching, you pull the wound cord, which releases from the main shaft. Then, you slide the handle off, and watch the top set off on its revolutionary journey. If you make several spinning tops, you can have battles with your friends to see whose stays spinning the longest.

The cord presents a strangulation risk if it is too long, and the handle is a choking risk to young children. Be careful with your designs and aware of the risks.

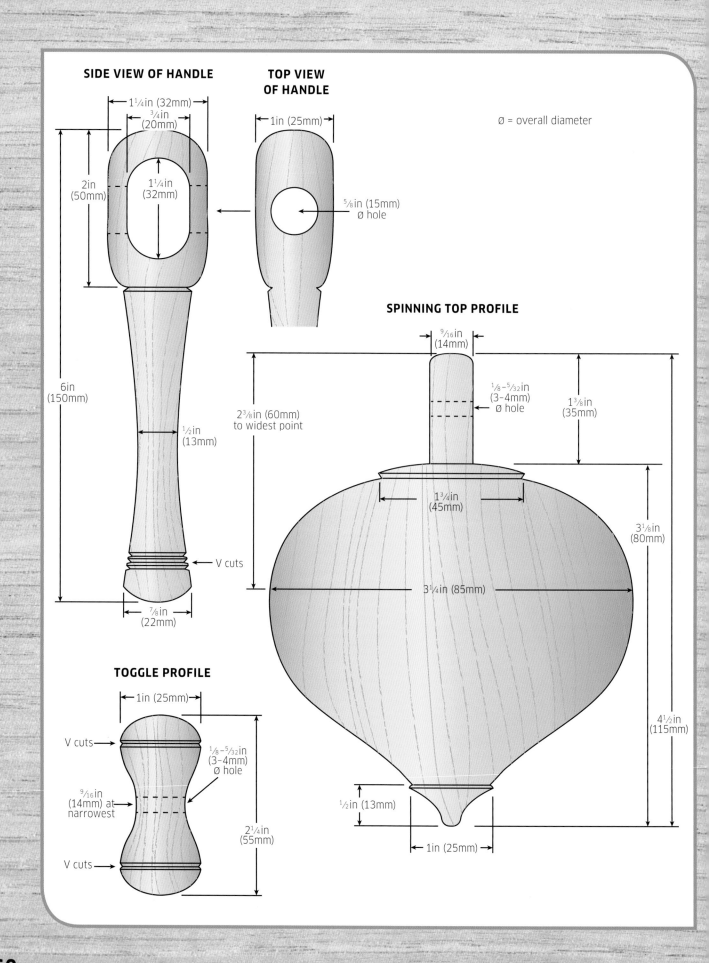

SIDE VIEW OF HANDLE

1¼in (32mm)

¾in (20mm)

2in (50mm)

1¼in (32mm)

6in (150mm)

½in (13mm)

V cuts

⅞in (22mm)

TOP VIEW OF HANDLE

1in (25mm)

⅝in (15mm) ø hole

ø = overall diameter

SPINNING TOP PROFILE

9/16in (14mm)

⅛–5/32in (3–4mm) ø hole

1⅜in (35mm)

1¾in (45mm)

3⅛in (80mm)

3¼in (85mm)

4½in (115mm)

½in (13mm)

1in (25mm)

2⅜in (60mm) to widest point

TOGGLE PROFILE

1in (25mm)

V cuts

⅛–5/32in (3–4mm) ø hole

9/16in (14mm) at narrowest

V cuts

2¼in (55mm)

11 Stopping just short of the main stem section, go back to the tailstock end and refine, gradually removing enough wood so that the tailstock can be removed. Then, you can refine the point.

12 Sand down to about 320 grit. Then, you need to decide how you want to decorate your spinning top. I favored rings of different colors, so I used the skew placed flat on the rest to create a series of grooves – more or less evenly spaced in this case.

13 Before coloring the rings, there is a useful trick you can use to prevent an indistinct transition from one color to the next. First, burn the lines using either wire held between two handles, or a thin piece of Formica or similar kitchen-surface laminate, to burn the V grooves. Then, sand the edge of the laminate to a V shape, holding the piece firmly and pressing it hard against the groove while the piece is rotating. You will need to keep creating a new edge on the laminate as the old one breaks down, but it works well.

14 You can use the lathe and toy-safe pens to color your top. With the lathe speed at about 300–500rpm, or slower if needed (too fast, and the nibs of the pens wear down and become useless), place the pen against the rotating work and color in the bands one by one. I chose a series of vivid colors that look dazzling when the top is spinning. When you are happy with the dome, remove the tailstock and turn away the remaining nub. Sand the top.

15 After coloring, use a combination of the spindle gouge and a beading and parting tool to shape the top curve of the main body of your spinning top. Remember to clean up and color this part before moving on to the top stem section.

16

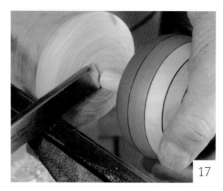

17

18

16 Use the beading and parting tool to create the stem. By setting the rest parallel, you can use your fingers as depth guides as you move the tool along the work. The stem needs to be just smaller than the ⅝-in. (15mm) hole created in the handle.

17 Once shaped, sand the stem and color it if you want to. Part off the piece from the lathe using successive cuts of the skew chisel or thin parting tool. Sand the end smooth, with a slight dome on it.

18 Now to create the toggle for the whip cord. I used pine (*Pinus* spp.) for this. I had a dowel of it already, which I mounted in the chuck, bringing up the tailstock for support. Measure and mark the length of the toggle, and use the spindle gouge to roughly shape it. Put a groove on the center line, and drill a ⅛-in. (3mm) hole through the center across the grain.

19

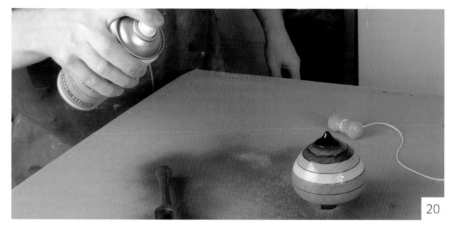

20

19 Shape the toggle with a nice cove and domed end. This required the removal of the tailstock to create fully. Cut a groove either end of the toggle, for some detail, then sand the toggle and refine the end. Part off from the small stub. Sand this stub smooth and to the shape required. Again, you can use toy-safe pens to color it.

20 Thread a length of cord through the hole in the toggle, and knot to secure in place. I placed the handle over the stem of the spinning top and measured the exact center of the window on the stem, before

drilling a ⅛-in. (3mm) hole through the stem to accept the cord. The main stem was colored black before all items were sprayed with a gloss lacquer. Once dry, you are ready to take your new toy for a spin.

Top tips

- Don't be afraid to experiment with shapes. Create smaller hand-spinning tops first to get the hang of things and see what shapes you like. The cost is lower material-wise if you do this.

- Try sanding the edges to create hexagonal, octagonal and other geometric shapes for the main body. This is especially good if you want to create spinning-top dice. You have to be accurate, though, or you will alter the center of gravity.

- These toys are not suitable for very young children. The hand-spinning tops have quite fine stems, and if you make them too fine they may snap if dropped. The whip cord is a potential strangulation risk and the handle a choking hazard.

- The longer the whip cord, the more speed you will generate when the top spins. There is a danger, however, that tops with very long cords will bounce all over the place before gaining equilibrium, so it is best to keep the whip cord to about 12 in. (300mm) long. I tried one longer and had great fun with the speed generated, but I could only use it outdoors as it bounced all over the place.

HOW TO MAKE THE TOP SPIN
Position the spinning top so that its balancing point is touching the floor. Pull the whip cord and slide the handle off to set the top spinning.

Skittles is a bowling game that has remained immensely popular in the UK through the years in its different forms. Whether it's in a skittle alley, fairground or ten-pin bowling complex, there's something compulsive about setting up the skittles, or pins, and knocking them down. A nicely turned set of wooden skittles means you can enjoy your own indoor or outdoor games at home.

Penguin skittles

Tools and materials

PPE: facemask/respirator

Drive spur and revolving center

Chuck

Calipers and gauges

Spindle roughing gouge

Beading and parting tool

Spindle gouge

Abrasives, 120–400 grit

Thin parting tool

Handsaw

Hammer

Pencil

Panel pin

Drill and bit

Paintbrushes

Primer

Gloss paint

Toy-safe pen

Angled scraper or skew chisel

Sphere-cutting jig (optional)

Creating ten skittles is an excellent exercise in copy turning. I used ash (*Fraxinus excelsior*), which is more open-grained than the other woods in this book but can withstand repeated hammering. The skittles are spindle-grain oriented work.

I thought it would be difficult to be original with the shape of skittles. They have to be top heavy, narrowing down in the lower section to a small base area that ensures the skittle will wobble easily or topple over when knocked. However, the basic shape suggested the idea of a penguin, and I developed a paint scheme to convey this comical bird. This in turn suggested ways in which I could alter the design a little, while still maintaining the necessary shape and balance. Paint and color are key factors in personalizing your work, so feel free to experiment. Watch the penguins at the zoo, then create your own stylized version.

All skittles need to have balls rolled at them, and snowballs seemed appropriate companion pieces for penguins. You can create the spheres by hand turning or using a purpose-made jig. Both methods work equally well. The snowballs are spindle-grain oriented projects, and should be turned from a close-grained hardwood: sycamore, beech, maple or similar.

Tip The paint offers sufficient protection to make splinters rare, but they can occur if the wood is hit hard. If this happens, just sand them off and repaint as necessary.

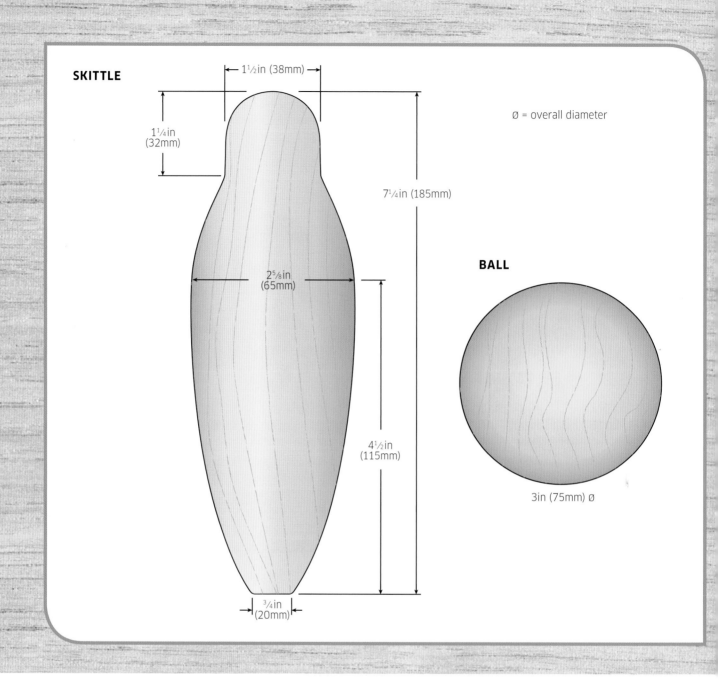

SKITTLE

1½in (38mm)

1¼in (32mm)

2⅝in (65mm)

¾in (20mm)

7¼in (185mm)

4½in (115mm)

Ø = overall diameter

BALL

3in (75mm) Ø

MAKING THE SKITTLES

1

1 One way to ensure accuracy and measure quickly is to cut a cardboard template or wooden stick with all the key positions marked. Cutting your first skittle to a pattern, however, is always tricky. I started by turning a skittle close to what was required, then I made some quick measurements and refined the shape to match the pattern as closely as I could. Once this first piece was created, I placed it up against the tool rest and marked the key body positions – length; the point where the head meets the shoulders; and the widest part of the skittle.

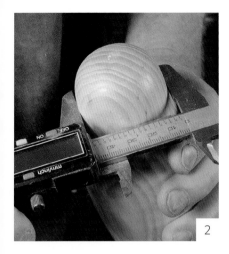

2

3

2 Use whatever calipers and gauges you have and set them to the relevant diameters, so that you can quickly work on the remaining skittles.

3 Mount your wood between centers. Use a spindle roughing gouge to create a cylinder just wider than the diameter required. Cut a spigot on the headstock end, and mount it in the lathe. Adjust the tool rest so that the marks fit inside the overall length of the wood used. The pieces I cut were too long, but any waste can be used for friction drives or jam chucks in other projects.

4

5

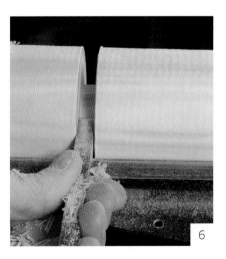

6

4 Use a beading and parting tool to create a tenon to suit the diameter of the penguin's head. Adjust until you have the right size, then elongate the tenon to match the mark on the tool rest that shows where the head meets the shoulders.

5 Use the beading and parting tool to make a parting cut to the depth of the widest part of the skittle, in line with your mark on the tool rest.

6 The last cut will be the one that defines the lowest section of the skittle. The right-hand side of the beading and parting tool is where the end of the skittle will be. The tenon is cut just larger than the diameter required for the base of the skittle. Don't cut this section any narrower, as you will need to clean up the head with no tailstock support before parting off the skittle.

7 Use a spindle gouge to adjust the area between the widest part of the body and the head. This should get the piece much closer to the shape required.

8 Once the top section is shaped, use the spindle roughing gouge to start removing the waste wood on the lower section.

9 Refine the lower section with the spindle gouge. Once you have formed the main shape, refine as required. The area where the penguin's head meets the shoulders needs to be slightly more defined than shown here. If you are not that confident with a spindle gouge, you could use an angled scraper or a skew on its side in scraping mode to refine the shape. The finish isn't as good as that from a gouge, but it will sand easily.

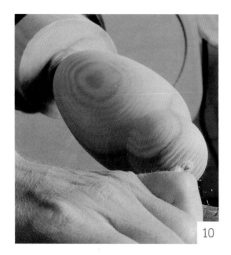

10 Once you are happy with the overall shape, remove the tailstock and revolving center. Clean up the head, then sand the skittle all over.

11 Reduce the lower tenon to the size required for the base. Refine the lowest section of the skittle to match the diameter of the tenon.

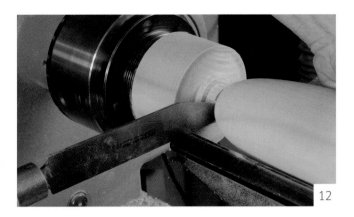

12 Part it off using a thin parting tool, or cut through with a handsaw while the lathe is stationary. Using the parting tool, I undercut very slightly so that the skittle sits on the very outer rim of the base. Create more skittles, as required.

13 Prime and undercoat the piece.

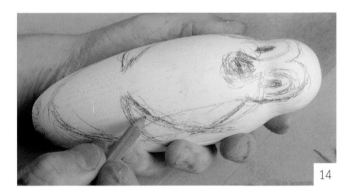

14 When dry, use a pencil to mark out your basic penguin paint design.

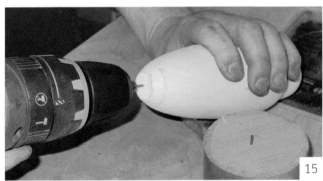

15 Nail a panel pin in a waste block of wood. Drill a hole in the base of the skittle the same diameter as the panel pin.

16 Mount the skittle on the waste block with the pin in it, so that you can paint it easily.

17 I used gloss paint for the main colors, followed by a toy-safe pen for the detail.

MAKING THE SNOWBALLS

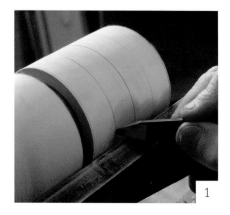

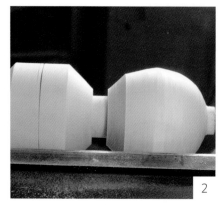

1 Turn a cylinder of wood to ⅛ in. (3mm) more than the diameter of sphere required for the balls. Cut a spigot on the end. Mount in a chuck on the lathe. Measure the diameter and mark on the cylinder. Mark the halfway position with a pencil, then mark halfway again between these halves. This will enable you to make the cuts to roughly shape the spheres.

2 The image above shows a piece mounted up with two spheres and their sections marked. On the left-hand sphere you can see the cuts that will enable you to refine the shape. On the sphere on the tailstock end, you can see how the cut form on the left half will guide you in creating the shape shown on the right half.

3 Use the spindle gouge to refine the shape of the sphere. Just be careful not to take too much off or the shape will be wrong. But if you leave too much waste wood in place, it makes the adjustment and final refinement later more tricky.

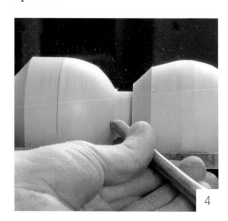

4 The handle movement, working from the center down to the lower sides, is quite pronounced. Once your sphere is roughly to shape, but just oversize, part it off.

5 Use a friction drive on the chuck and one on the tailstock. Depending on the revolving center, you can have an over-fit or a screw-on version of this support. As long as they run true and support the sphere properly, it doesn't matter. Use the spindle gouge to refine the shape of your sphere.

6 As the sphere rotates, you will see a fuzzy outer shadow shape where the sphere is uneven, and an inner solid section. Remove the fuzzy shape when you are cutting so you cut to the solid section. Once done, stop the lathe, release the pressure between centers and rotate the ball so that a fresh area can be refined.

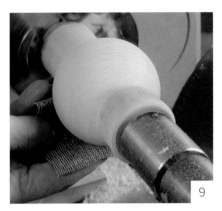

7 Here, you can see how I had some waste wood to remove due to there being a shoulder of wood. This was the flat area that had been left when I parted it off.

8 It doesn't matter whether you use a gouge or a scraper, just work a section. Rotate the ball all the way round until you have your perfect sphere.

9 Sand the ball, rotating the sphere as each area is finished. Once complete, repeat this whole process for the other balls.

Using a sphere-cutting jig

To create a sphere from a cylinder of wood, you can use a sphere-cutting jig like the one shown here. However, you will still need to use the friction drive method to hold the ball (see Step 5) to clean it up. The beauty of using a specialist jig is the accuracy; the ease of use; and the knowledge that, once everything is set up, micro-adjustments are easy, with everything locked in place and controllable. This minimizes problems such as catches. Which route you take is probably dependent on how many spheres you are likely to cut. Whatever method you use, you can still end up with the same result.

With a jig, the process of cutting a sphere is almost identical to hand turning, but it allows for precise micro-adjustments, making the final refinement much easier.

Throwing quoits, or rings, over columns set at different positions and distances away from the player is a traditional game that makes for exciting competition. It also brings to mind all the fun of the fair, along with all the frustration of near misses just when the prize seems in sight.

Snowman quoits

Tools and materials

PPE: facemask/respirator

Drive spur and revolving center

Chuck

Beading and parting tool

Thin parting tool

Spindle roughing gouge

Spindle gouge

Abrasives, 120–400 grit

Bowl gouge

Skew chisel

Disc sander (optional)

Random orbital sander (optional)

Paintbrushes

Primer

Gloss or satin paint

Toy-safe pens

This project has three freestanding columns, which can be moved to any position and distance. To make it a nice companion game to the Penguin Skittles, and to reflect the love all children have for snow, I have designed the columns as stylized snowmen.

These snowmen need to be stable and to remain standing when hit by the quoits, so I have given them square bases. The snowmen can be made out of any suitable hardwood, and I used sycamore (*Acer pseudoplatanus*) once again. It is durable and easy to turn, paint and color as required.

The rings were problematic in terms of their strength. To create something in solid wood that is not prone to snapping due to short sections of end grain might mean that they become too heavy if you increase the thickness and width of the wood to counter this problem. So, once again I decided to use high-quality, laminated birch-faced ply. It is strong and, because the ply is made of layers of wooden veneers presented at different angles to each other, it won't break, even in smaller sections, as long as the laminates are oriented in the right direction. Just cut the rings from the face of the ply and the laminates will lie across the ring, giving the ring excellent strength.

Tip Instead of turning the throwing rings, you could buy rubber, plastic or rope ones to use instead. These are available from many toy stores and the internet.

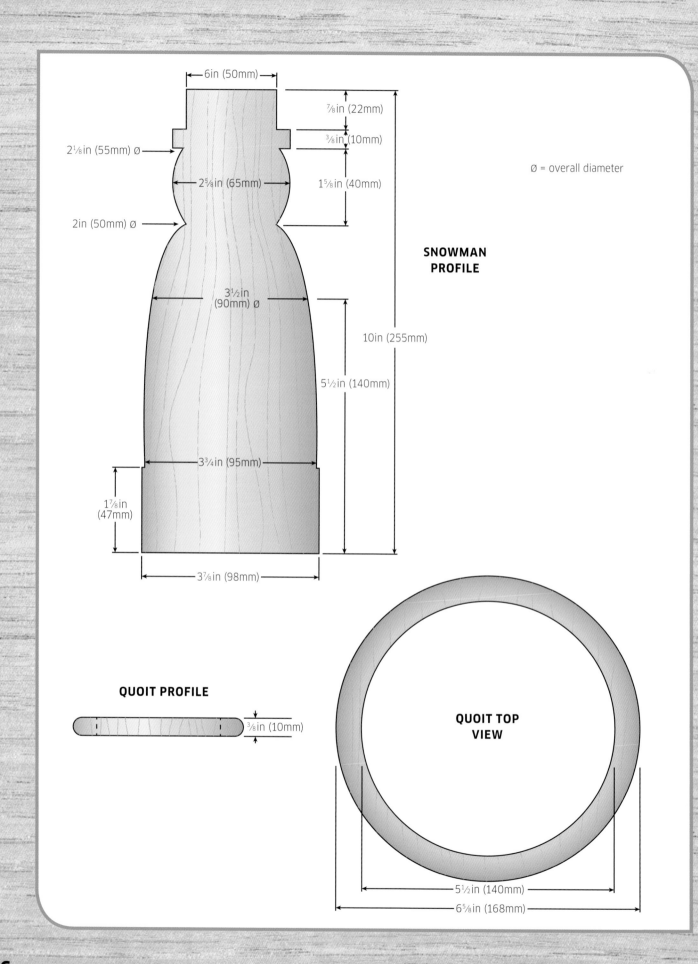

SNOWMAN PROFILE

6in (50mm)

⅞in (22mm)

⅜in (10mm)

2⅛in (55mm) Ø

2⅝in (65mm)

1⅝in (40mm)

2in (50mm) Ø

Ø = overall diameter

3½in (90mm) Ø

10in (255mm)

5½in (140mm)

3¾in (95mm)

1⅞in (47mm)

3⅞in (98mm)

QUOIT PROFILE

⅜in (10mm)

QUOIT TOP VIEW

5½in (140mm)

6⅝in (168mm)

MAKING THE SNOWMEN

1 Working with a square section of wood, cut just over length to allow for a spigot to be cut at one end. Mount between centers. Use a beading and parting tool to cut the spigot on the tailstock end to fit your chuck. Then, measure up to the height required for the square, lower section of the snowman. Using a thin parting tool, cut into the square corners and down through them, stopping when you meet the solid inner section.

2 Stop the lathe, remove the wood from the lathe and mount the spigot in the chuck. Use a spindle roughing gouge to block in the shape to the widest diameter required for the snowman, leaving the square base section alone. Note the square shoulders at the lowest part. Be wary of these when working. Once you have a cylinder, make a parting cut where the top of the snowman's body will be. Cut to a depth that can be deepened later on, but shows clearly where you need to refine the body and head section.

3 Use a spindle gouge to reduce the top section. I am using a pull cut here rather than a push cut. This is crude and may damage the surface, but it removes wood quickly.

4 Measure and mark the position of the head section. Use the spindle gouge to roughly shape the head.

5 Use the beading and parting tool to make a parting cut to the depth of the widest part of the snowman, in line with the mark on the tool rest.

6 The body and head need refining according to the pattern, so I marked the relevant positions on the tool rest, using the same technique as for the Penguin skittles (see page 68). Refine the body and head forms so that everything works in balance and proportion, and then sand.

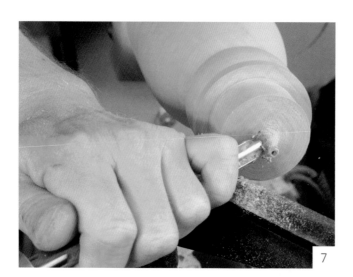

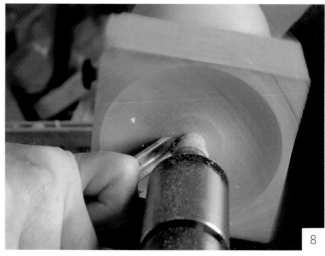

7 Remove the tailstock, and remove the waste wood not needed for the hat. Then, use the spindle gouge to clean up the top. Multiple light cuts are best, due to the extended overhang of the work from the chuck.

8 Remove the piece from the chuck, reverse it and hold the hat gently in the chuck jaws. Bring up the revolving center to centralize everything and lock the piece in place. Undercut the base, leaving a solid outer rim so that the snowman is stable when placed on a surface. Remove the snowman from the lathe and carve off the nub left under the center. Sand the underside smooth. Now make two more snowmen to match the first.

MAKING THE QUOITS

1 The block of ply for the quoits is laminated so that the ply is mainly faceplate-grain oriented. Mount between centers. (You can instead drill a hole and mount the block on a screwchuck or faceplate, using the tailstock to provide extra support.) Use a bowl gouge to true up the face and edge.

2 Cut from both sides on the edge, so you don't break off any splinters on the top and bottom faces. Reduce the diameter of the block to the size needed for the quoits.

3 With the block mounted between centers, use the thin parting tool to make a few plunge cuts to create a spigot that fits in the chuck. Once cut, remove the block from the lathe and mount on the chuck.

4 Using the tailstock for support where you can, measure and mark the thickness of the rings required for the quoits.

5 Use the thin parting tool to part in to about 1-in. (25mm) depth on the first ring.

6 Lay a skew on its side and use a scraping move to create a pronounced V chamfer on the two corners created by the parting cut. I also chamfered the top corner.

7 Repeat the process to make as many ring sections as required. In this case, I thought five rings would be enough.

8 Clean up the top face with a little skim cut, and sand the outer ring edges. You could round them over, but as long as there are no sharp corners this shape will work fine.

9 Once sanded, use the thin parting tool to plunge cut just enough into the face of the ply to release the first ring.

10 Sand the flat face of the next ring, then release the next one, and so on, until you have your complete set of rings.

FINISHING OFF

1 Take the snowmen and sand the square shoulders on a disc sander or by rubbing them on an abrasive strip on a flat surface. I am using 320 grit here.

2 Sand the top of the hat, but be careful, because if you get the angle of attack wrong, you will end up with an irregularly shaped hat.

3 Sand the non-sanded face of the quoits by using a random orbital sander, or by hand.

4 Coat everything with a primer before applying gloss or satin paint as desired. I used toy-safe pens for some of the fine detail.

Top tips

• Since the quoits will hit the snowmen, make sure you use dense, close-grained material for the snowmen to minimize any damage and splinter risks.

• To further minimize splinter risk and damage, don't have any fine detail on the snowmen. Keep everything a good size and boldly shaped.

• Instead of making snowmen, you could make Christmas trees. Round the tops slightly to make sure there are no sharp points. Experiment with the shapes and make something unique.

Magic tricks are a visual treat when performed well, and there is the added challenge of trying to figure out just how they work. This particular trick has been around for a very long time and was certainly something that caught me out when I was younger. It is quite a simple trick, but only when you know how!

Disappearing ball trick

Tools and materials

PPE: facemask/respirator

Drive spur and revolving center

Chuck

Spindle gouge

Thin parting tool

Scraper or shear scraper

Spindle roughing gouge

Beading and parting tool

Round-nose or French curve scraper

Abrasives, 120–400 grit

Bead forming tool, 3⁄16 in. (5mm)

Sphere-cutting jig (optional)

Angled scraper or skew chisel

Dye or stain

Satin lacquer

This is a four-part, spindle-grain project that will test your skills in working to fine tolerances and disguising the joins. To help with this, you need to have some detail that will hide and obfuscate what is going on when various parts of the trick are lifted.

The cup has a hollow interior, into which is placed a loose ball. Over this is placed a false cap that fits on top of the ball – it has a hollow underneath, while the top is shaped and colored to look just like the loose ball. Therein lies the illusion at the heart of the trick. Over the top of this, the lid is fitted.

For this project, it is important to work in clear stages, and to constantly check measurements and fit. It's vital that the wood selected holds fine detail and has a very fine, almost indiscernible, grain structure. I chose sycamore (*Acer pseudoplatanus*), but walnut (*Juglans* spp.), boxwood (*Buxus* spp.) or fruitwoods would work well.

Tip When refining the shapes with a scraper or a skew chisel in scraping mode, remember that delicate, light cuts will help you to achieve a nice, clean finish that requires minimal sanding.

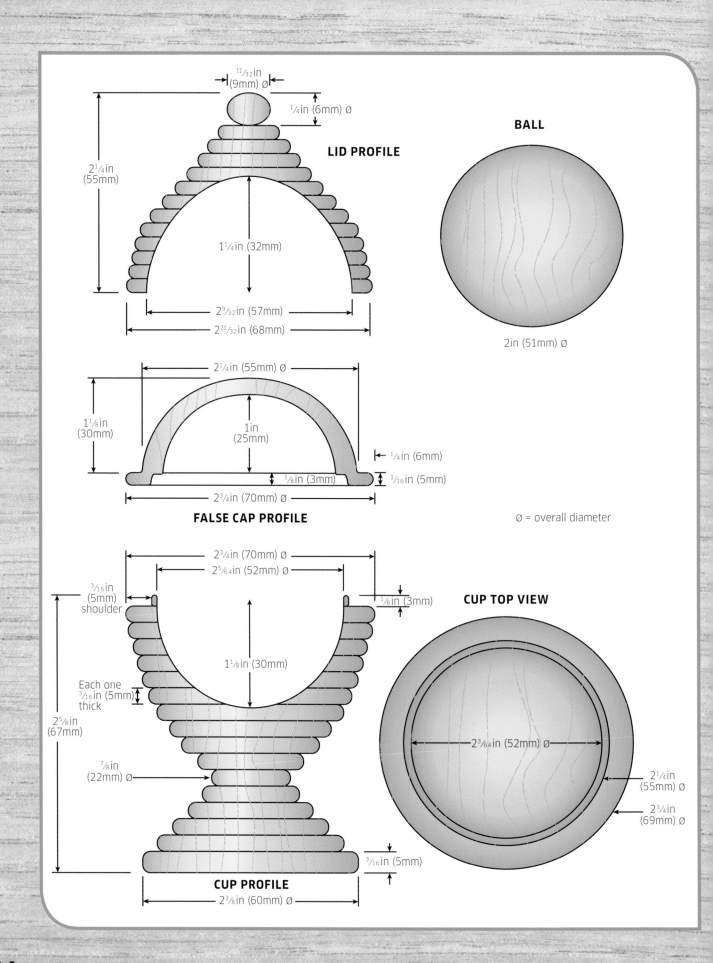

$^{11}/_{32}$in (9mm) ∅

$^{1}/_{4}$in (6mm) ∅

LID PROFILE

2$^{1}/_{4}$in (55mm)

1$^{1}/_{4}$in (32mm)

2$^{9}/_{32}$in (57mm)

2$^{21}/_{32}$in (68mm)

BALL

2in (51mm) ∅

2$^{1}/_{4}$in (55mm) ∅

1$^{1}/_{8}$in (30mm)

1in (25mm)

$^{1}/_{4}$in (6mm)

$^{1}/_{8}$in (3mm)

$^{3}/_{16}$in (5mm)

2$^{3}/_{4}$in (70mm) ∅

FALSE CAP PROFILE

∅ = overall diameter

2$^{3}/_{4}$in (70mm) ∅

2$^{5}/_{64}$in (52mm) ∅

$^{3}/_{16}$in (5mm) shoulder

$^{1}/_{8}$in (3mm)

CUP TOP VIEW

1$^{1}/_{8}$in (30mm)

Each one $^{3}/_{16}$in (5mm) thick

2$^{5}/_{8}$in (67mm)

$^{7}/_{8}$in (22mm) ∅

2$^{3}/_{64}$in (52mm) ∅

2$^{1}/_{4}$in (55mm) ∅

2$^{3}/_{4}$in (69mm) ∅

$^{3}/_{16}$in (5mm)

CUP PROFILE

2$^{3}/_{8}$in (60mm) ∅

MAKING THE CUP AND LID

1 Mount the wood between centers, and use a spindle roughing gouge to turn to a cylinder of the right size. Cut a spigot at one end, then mount in the chuck. Using a spindle gouge, create a slightly elongated egg form.

2 The end near the chuck will become the cup section, and the upper egg-shaped part will become the lid. On the center line of the shape, use a thin parting tool to cut a small spigot. Part off the lid.

3 Hollow the inside of the cup. I used the same hollowing technique as in the Wooden puzzle (see page 37) but you might need either a multi-tipped tool with a round or teardrop-shaped cutter, or a round-nose or French curve scraper to refine the shape. The hollow needs to be hemispherical, to accept the ball. You can use a template for this. Later – when you have created your ball – if you find that the hollow is slightly out, you can remount the cup and adjust the hollow.

4 Remove the bulk of the waste with the spindle gouge. Use a scraper or shear scraper to clean up the inside. Once the cup is shaped, sand the inside then gently sand the inner and outer edges of the spigot.

5 If you are unfamiliar with cutting hollows to a specific size, you can make a ply or paper template to check the shape. If the hollow matches, then all is well. If it is slightly tight, as in this case, you can remount the piece and adjust. If the hollow is too big, you can either make a new cup or just increase the size of the sphere and the corresponding hollow in the false cap.

6 Use a bead forming tool to cut some beads in the cup – not to full depth at this stage. You can cut them by hand, but that will be tricky on this shape. A forming tool will give the same width and shape every time. You have to control the depth of cut, so make sure the crowns of the beads flow visually. They should have no highs and lows.

MAKING THE BALL

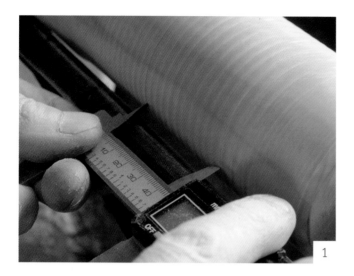

1 The ball needs to be a tight fit, but easily removed. Use the same method for this as for the balls in the Penguin skittles project (see page 72). Carefully measure the maximum width of the ball, and create a cylinder just slightly larger in diameter. Mount the cylinder in the lathe, bring up the tailstock and mark the width of the ball. I noticed a small flaw in the end of the cylinder, hence my marking it well in from the end.

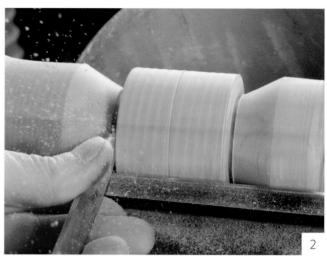

2 Part down either end. You can see that I added $5/64$ in. (2mm) or so at either end to allow for clean-up later. If you mark everything exactly, it removes your margin for error. Mark the center. Divide each half in two, and mark those positions.

3 Using the spindle gouge, partially turn the outer quadrants so that you have a flat on them. Don't make these too steep, or you will remove some of the wood you wish to keep.

4 Start to refine the shape, working on either side from the top down to the parting cuts. Then, part or cut off the partially shaped sphere.

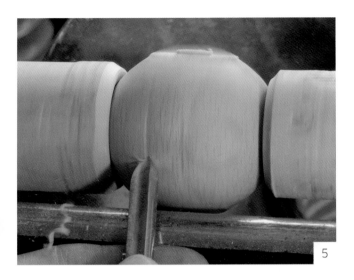

5 Fix the sphere between two friction drives purpose-made to hold spheres, mounting it so that the square ends are vertical. Refine the shape. Note the square end – it is quite large and the sphere shape is not quite right. This shows my mistake. While the length of the sphere was right, and I got to the correct sphere diameter from this, I forgot to adjust the width to match the length. To correct this, I had to make extra cuts all the way round to get to the right diameter.

6 Remember to turn the ball frequently, so that you get a nice even form. If you are micro-adjusting the form, an angled scraper or skew chisel laid on its side in scraping mode will work well.

7 Once shaped, sand the sphere all over and check for fit in the cup you have already created. Can you see here how it sits a little high? If this happens, remount the sphere and adjust until it sits neatly in the hollow.

MAKING THE FALSE CAP

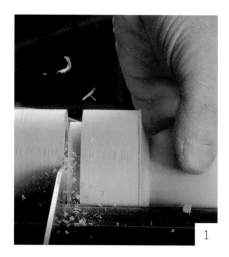

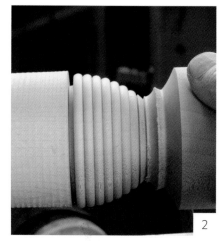

1 Take the cylinder of wood that contains the lid, and mount the tailstock end in your chuck. Cut a spigot to suit your chuck jaws, in a position that leaves a section longer than is required for the finished lid. Part off the lid, leaving the spigot on that part.

2 The section remaining in the chuck will be used for the false cap. This form must sit over the loose ball while its upper surface mimics a hollow half-ball. When the cup is placed against the cylinder, the false cap is slightly wider than the maximum width of the top of the cup.

3 Measure the outer diameter of the spigot on the cup, and transfer this onto the tailstock end of the false cap. This marks the outer edges of the recess needed to join the false cap onto the top of the cup.

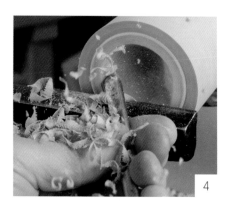

4 Hollow out the bulk of the inside hollow, but stop about ¼ in. (6mm) short of the marked recess width.

5 Use the skew chisel on its side, with the long point on the outer side of the blade, to create the recess to width and depth. Then, refine the inside of the hollow, checking that the ball fits snugly inside but can be easily removed. Fit the ball in the cup and bring up the cup and ball to fit against the false cap, to double-check everything. If there are any errors at this stage, you will find it hard to backtrack.

6 Here is the tricky bit. You need to have as thin a wall thickness on the false cap as possible, but you must avoid breaking through the square lower corner of the recess. You also need to mimic the shape and size of the loose ball as closely as possible, without making the wall so thin as to be fragile. Get the shape and size wrong, and people will quickly spot the difference between the false cap and the loose ball. The thin parting tool will help make a fine cut to depth.

7 Use the spindle gouge to refine the exterior shape of the dome.

8 Once you get close to the final shape, use a scraper or a skew chisel in scraping mode for your fine adjustments. Be aware that scraping can produce grain tear-out. Delicate, light cuts will help you to achieve a nice, clean finish that requires minimal sanding.

9 Place the cup up against the false cap. You already know the loose ball fits; now check that everything looks right.

10 Make adjustments to the false cap as required.

11 Cut off the false cap through the waste section, and use the waste section to create a jam chuck with a spigot on the tailstock end to lock into the recess in the false cap. Clean up the top, using the spindle gouge to deal with the small nub of wood. Sand it.

FINISHING OFF

1 Mount the lid in the chuck. Measure the width of the largest outer diameter of the sphere cut on the false cap, and transfer this diameter to the underside of the lid.

2 Remove the bulk of the waste with the spindle gouge, using the same end-grain hollowing technique as before. Refine the inside with a scraper but stop shy of the maximum width required.

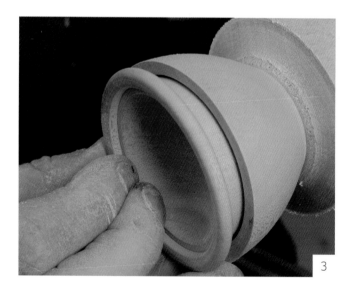

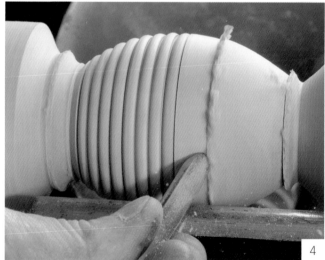

3 Regularly place the false cap into the hollow to check for a good fit. You need to be able to lift off the lid with one hand without touching the false cap. Sand the inside of the hollow.

4 Remove the lid from the chuck and fit the cup in place. Place the false cap on to the cup, then the lid on top of this, and bring up the tailstock. Using the spindle gouge, refine the outer shape to get the curvature and width of the pieces flowing together.

5 Use the bead forming tool – or if you are cutting the outer detail by hand, a tool that will allow you to do that – to form the beads as far as you can on the plain sections exposed. Pay particular attention to the joins. Make sure that you get clean cuts, with the grooved lower sections of the beads right on the joins. Don't leave any steps or scores in areas that will be visible.

6 Use the spindle gouge to refine the very top of the lid. Again, use a bead forming tool to create beads, staying just shy of parting through at the top of the bead. Stop the lathe and remove the waste with a carving tool. Sand the top of the bead.

7 Now you need to finish off the cup. First, cut more beads.

Tip V cuts, stepped pyramid-like details or beads work very well to disguise the joins in this project, but the wall thickness needs to allow for this. Also, make sure that each detail has uniform width, spacing and depth, so that you cannot see any irregularities.

8

9

8 Then, refine the base part of the cup, and bead that area before sanding and parting it off.

9 Color the parts. I dyed all the surfaces black, except for the ball and the outer dome of the false cap. Black disguises joins well. I used red for the ball and for the part of the cap that masquerades as the ball, because this stands out well against the black. Once dry, I coated the dye with a satin lacquer.

10

10 It is worth noting that on the false cap, I did not replicate exactly the raised spigot section seen on the cup in which the ball sits. Some of the older versions of this trick do have it, some do not. You can copy this detail and have a perfect match, but most people won't notice this slight discrepancy.

The trick

Start the trick with all the pieces in place. Then, pick up the lid and the false cap as one unit. Do not separate the two parts; keep them tight in one hand. You have revealed the loose ball in the cup. Now, remove the ball and place it in your pocket. Replace the lid and false cap on top of the empty cup. After a little theatrical 'business' and a few magic words, lift only the lid, leaving the false cap in place to suggest that the ball has magically returned. The surprise should be sufficient to dupe most victims, although the success of the trick will depend on both your conjuring and turning skills!

Left shows the assembled trick; below shows all four parts, including the ball and false cap.

I remember fondly the toy train I had as a child. There were loose building blocks in the carriages, so that you also had the pleasure of building things when the train arrived at its destination. This is a multi-part project that creates a stylized version of an old steam train. I have broken the sequence of making and assembling into different stages, to make things easier to follow.

Pull-along train

Toy trains are hard to make solely by turning. The turned parts are all spindle-grain oriented wood, but I have had to introduce some square-section undercarriage parts to hold the axles and wheels. This toy is quite large, but you can scale it down if you prefer.

The wood is a combination of poplar (*Populus* sp.), high-quality laminated birch-faced ply, sycamore (*Acer pseudoplatanus*) and a bought hardwood dowel (for the wheel axles), which saved time and was cheaper for the size of lumber. Other woods are also suitable, but the ones I used allowed me to get fine detail as well as being easy to color.

Tools and materials

PPE: facemask/respirator

Drive spur and revolving center

Chuck

Spindle roughing gouge

Spindle gouge

Bead forming tool, ⅛ in. (3mm)

Abrasives, 120–400 grit

Thin parting tool

Handsaw

Bowl gouge

Sawtooth bit

Drill chuck

Forceps, shear sander, sanding arbor or sanding ball

Chisel

Disc sander

Drill bits, ½ in. (13mm) and 2¼–2⅜ in. (58–60mm)

Paper towel

Depth gauge

Beading and parting tool

Skew chisel

Adhesive: PVA and epoxy resin

Clamps

Hot-melt glue

Dowel rods, ½ in. (13mm)

Calipers

Bandsaw

Drill press

Rare-earth magnets, ¾ x ⅛ in. (20 x 3mm)

Round-head threaded carriage bolts

Primer

Toy-safe paint or dye

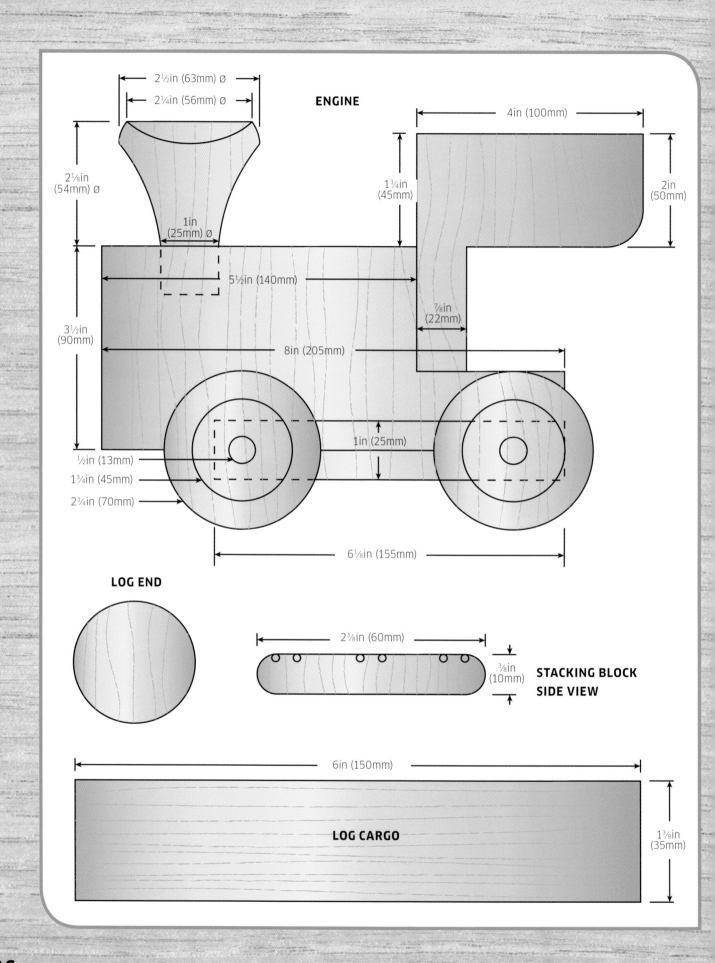

ENGINE

2½in (63mm) ∅

2¼in (56mm) ∅

2⅛in (54mm) ∅

1in (25mm) ∅

4in (100mm)

1¾in (45mm)

2in (50mm)

5½in (140mm)

⅞in (22mm)

3½in (90mm)

8in (205mm)

1in (25mm)

½in (13mm)

1¾in (45mm)

2¾in (70mm)

6⅛in (155mm)

LOG END

2⅜in (60mm)

⅜in (10mm)

STACKING BLOCK
SIDE VIEW

6in (150mm)

LOG CARGO

1⅜in (35mm)

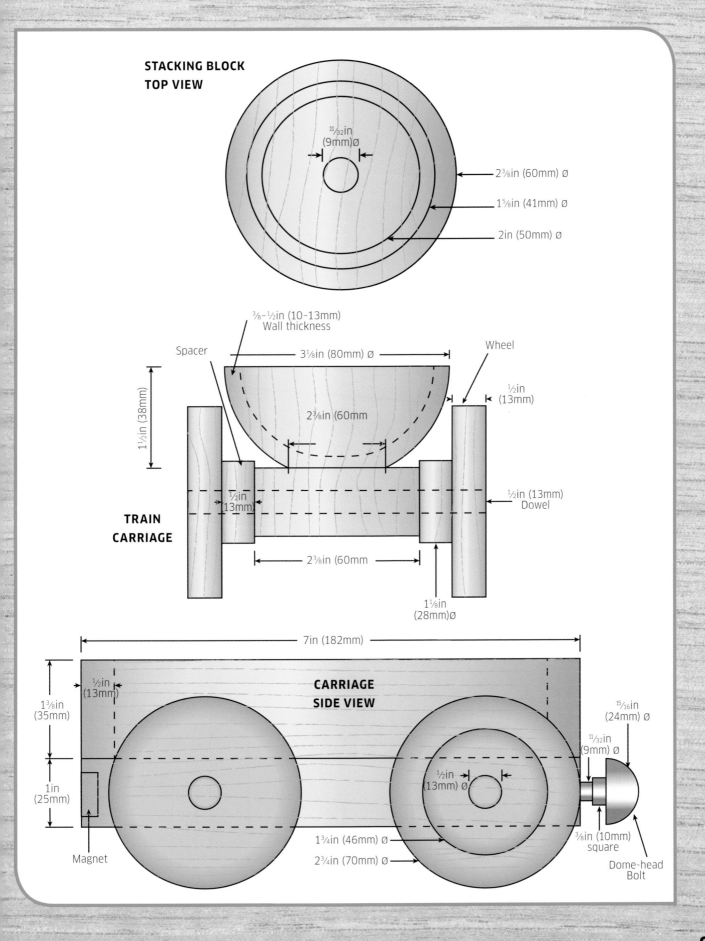

**STACKING BLOCK
TOP VIEW**

$^{11}/_{32}$in
(9mm)Ø

2$^{3}/_{8}$in (60mm) Ø

1$^{5}/_{8}$in (41mm) Ø

2in (50mm) Ø

$^{3}/_{8}$–$^{1}/_{2}$in (10–13mm)
Wall thickness

Spacer

3$^{1}/_{8}$in (80mm) Ø

Wheel

$^{1}/_{2}$in
(13mm)

2$^{3}/_{8}$in (60mm)

1$^{1}/_{2}$in (38mm)

$^{1}/_{2}$in
13mm)

$^{1}/_{2}$in (13mm)
Dowel

**TRAIN
CARRIAGE**

2$^{3}/_{8}$in (60mm)

1$^{1}/_{8}$in
(28mm)Ø

7in (182mm)

$^{1}/_{2}$in
(13mm)

1$^{3}/_{8}$in
(35mm)

**CARRIAGE
SIDE VIEW**

$^{15}/_{16}$in
(24mm) Ø

$^{11}/_{32}$in
(9mm) Ø

$^{1}/_{2}$in
(13mm) Ø

1in
(25mm)

Magnet

1$^{3}/_{4}$in (46mm) Ø

2$^{3}/_{4}$in (70mm) Ø

$^{3}/_{8}$in (10mm)
square

Dome-head
Bolt

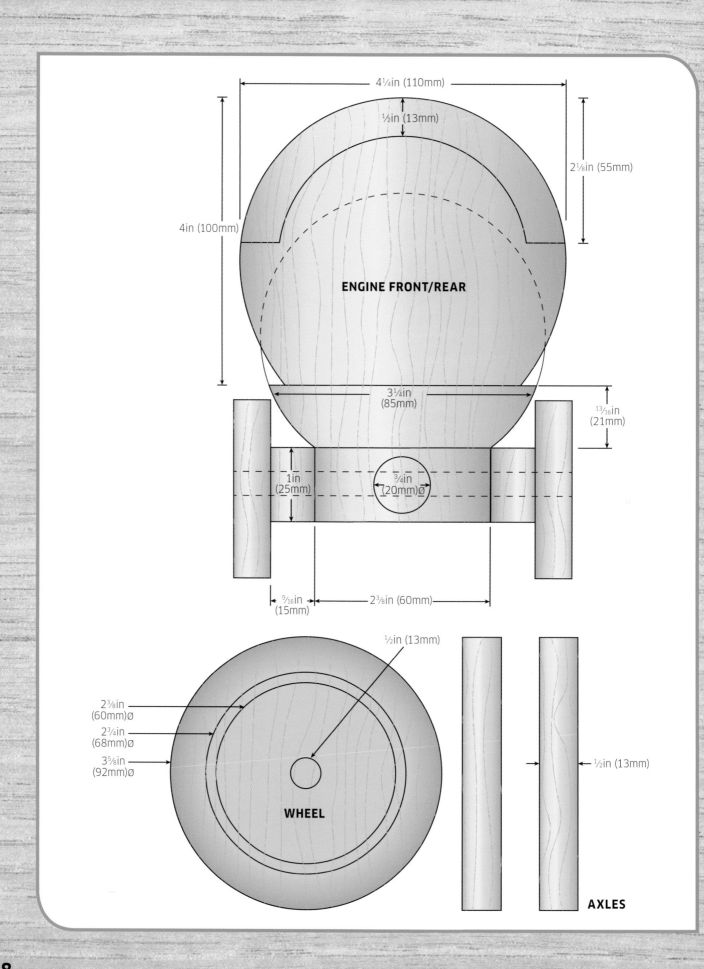

4¼in (110mm)

½in (13mm)

2⅛in (55mm)

4in (100mm)

ENGINE FRONT/REAR

3¼in (85mm)

¹³⁄₁₆in (21mm)

1in (25mm)

¾in (20mm)ø

⁹⁄₁₆in (15mm)

2⅜in (60mm)

½in (13mm)

2⅜in (60mm)ø

2¾in (68mm)ø

3⅝in (92mm)ø

WHEEL

½in (13mm)

AXLES

MAKING THE ENGINE

1 The engine is essentially just a cylinder of wood – poplar in this case. Mount between centers, and use a spindle roughing gouge to turn to size. Cut a spigot at one end, then mount in the chuck. This leaves what will be the front end of the engine free for you to clean off the center marks and add some detail. A spindle gouge is ideal for this. The central area has a button-shaped dome.

2 At the widest part of the dome, cut a bead using a bead forming tool. You can also use a gouge, parting tool or skew in scraping mode for this. The outer section of the end is flat across with a slight chamfer on the corner.

3 Sand the piece. Measure and mark the length required, and part or saw the cylinder off. When cutting any distance into wood with a parting tool, remove the blade frequently to remove debris to prevent it from binding. Also when cutting deep, to further minimize the risk of binding, make a clearance cut in the waste wood area to widen the parting tool clearance gap.

Tip When power-sanding, move the arbor across the work with a very fluid motion. Poplar is particularly soft and you can quickly create sanding hollows that will mar the surface.

MAKING THE CAB

1 The cab will be modified later to fit onto the engine. It is a large piece, so I used laminated birch-faced ply as the most cost-effective material. The ply is laminated so that it looks like spindle-oriented grain. Use a bowl gouge to turn a cylinder. Ply is abrasive and can be tough turning, so a bowl gouge – being stronger than a spindle roughing gouge or spindle gouge – is ideal. Cut a spigot at one end to fit your chuck.

2 Sand the cylinder and mount it in the chuck. Now, you need to create a wide hole in it. I drilled this with a sawtooth bit held in a drill chuck in the tailstock. The hole is quite deep, but could just about be hollowed with the end-grain hollowing techniques used in previous projects. Your other option is to use a multi-tipped hollowing and scraping tool to hollow the inside. This allows you to use a small scraper tip to remove the waste, and a large tip to clean up and refine the hollow. High-quality drill bits can be expensive, so the choice is yours.

3 Once you have the hollow to the right depth, and an even wall thickness, sand the piece. It is not advisable to stick your hands in the hollow. Instead, use forceps holding abrasive; a shear sander; a sanding arbor in a drill, with an extension rod; or a sanding ball.

4 Cut off the piece to the length required, leaving enough thickness at the bottom to form the front wall. You need to cut away part of the side wall to create the arched cover form. Either use a handsaw to cut away the waste, or hold the cylinder in a suitable cradle – secured with clamps – and use a bandsaw. You need to end up with the solid end and half the arched side wall. Use a chisel and abrasives to clean up any stray bits.

5 A disc sander helps with sanding and shaping the end section, but is not essential: you can use hand-held abrasives to do this instead. Make sure everything is smooth, and round over the lower cut corners of the cab ready for painting. There will be a score line and a center hole left from the drill bit. These can be filled or left as you choose.

MAKING THE CARRIAGES

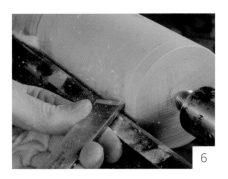

1 To make the carriages, turn a cylinder of wood between centers and cut a spigot at one end. Mount in the chuck, clamping on to the spigot. Either drill a hole the right size to the depth required – in this case a 2¼–2⅜-in. (58–60mm) wide hole some 6 in. (150mm) deep; or use a multi-tipped hollowing tool of the right size and heft, with a small tip to remove waste and a larger one to clean things up.

2 Use a depth gauge to measure how far you have got. Repeat the hollowing process until you get to the correct depth, then sand the inside.

3 The walls of the carriages need to be about ½ in. (13mm) thick. Use a thin parting tool to part off ½ in. (13mm) longer than the bored hole. Part the piece almost all the way through, stopping just short so that you can cut off the cylinder with a handsaw while the lathe is stationary.

4 Using the waste wood that is already in the chuck, cut a spigot that fits very tightly in the open end of the cylinder. A beading and parting tool or just a parting tool will make light work of this.

5 Test for fit regularly; this needs to fit well. This section will create an end-cap for the cylinder.

6 Having cut very slightly too loose, I remedied the problem by placing a layer of paper towel over the spigot before pushing on the cylinder. Bring up the tailstock for support, applying only light pressure to avoid marking the end. Use a skew in scraping mode to make a V cut ½ in. (13mm) in from the tailstock end, then another on the other end right on top of the join.

7 Sand the piece and remove the cylinder. Clean up the end of the spigot on the piece left in the lathe, and trim the spigot to about ¼ in. (6mm) in depth. Note that I put a mark ½ in. (13mm) in from the shoulder of the end-cap.

8 Using the thin parting tool, part the end-cap off.

9 Put some adhesive on the end-cap spigot. Clamp the end-cap in place, and leave it to set.

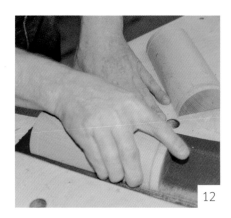

10 Once set, cut the piece in half lengthwise. Note the quadrant on the lower inside edge near the fence. It is hot-melt glued in position to provide stability and support, stopping the cylinder from rolling in the cut. The push stick provides forward and side pressure and the hand provides extra support behind the blade. Also note the two grooves you cut in step 6. They add a bit of detail and disguise the end-cap join.

11 The result should be two nicely hollowed carriages.

12 Sand the top faces smooth, using abrasive laid on a flat surface. Sand and radius slightly all the remaining sharp edges.

MAKING THE LOGS AND STACKING DISCS

1 For the logs, mount the wood between centers and create a cylinder to the diameter required. Sand, cut to length off the lathe, and sand the ends. To make the stacking discs, create a cylinder of the required diameter between centers, cut a spigot both ends and mount the cylinder in a chuck. With the tailstock for support, use the spindle gouge, beading and parting tool or bead forming tool to create evenly spaced beads for the rounded outer edges.

2 I wanted the discs to have round edges and to all be the same size. You can vary this, but for my needs the easiest option was to use a bead forming tool. There was a gap the width of my thin parting tool between discs, so I could run it down between the formed edges and cut them off cleanly to size. This resulted in minimal sanding.

3 Form all the discs with the bead forming tool. Then, just under halfway from the headstock, part almost all the way through a gap between two of the rings. Stop the lathe, remove the tailstock and saw though to remove the tailstock end section.

4 After the end piece has been removed, use the spindle gouge to clean up the outer face.

5 Using the bead forming tool, spindle gouge or skew in scraping mode, cut some decoration on the outer face. I chose a bead forming tool for two beads. I made the first bead near the center.

6 Make the second bead near the outer edge.

MAKING THE WHEELS AND SPACERS

1 The 12 wheels are created in a very similar way to the stacking discs. Turn a cylinder between centers, close to the required diameter. Cut a spigot at one or both ends and mount it in the lathe. Using the skew or spindle roughing gouge, true the cylinder up to the right diameter. Roughly sand it.

2 You need to accurately bore a central hole in the cylinder that will allow a tight fit on the dowel being used for the axle. You can turn the axle, but I bought 1/2-in. (13mm) dowel rods. Using a drill chuck fitted in the headstock, with a drill bit to suit the dowel size, bore a hole in the cylinder the depth of the twist on the bit. Extract the bit regularly to clear the shavings.

3 Once drilled, use the spindle gouge to clean up the face. Using the long point of the skew in scraping mode, I put a groove near the outer edge to add detail. This also acted as a barrier that I could work up to.

4 Using the spindle gouge or skew in scraping mode, depress the inner section of the wheel by 1/32 in. (1mm) or so. Again, this was done to add detail to the wheel.

5 Using calipers, mark the width of the wheel.

6 Using the thin parting tool, part off the marked wheel. Repeat the process until you have made all 12 wheels.

7 For the spacers, there are two widths required. One size fits the carriages, and the other fits the wheels on the engine. Create a cylinder of the required diameter and mount it in the chuck. Drill a hole that is suitable for the axle.

8 Measure the width of the spacers required. Note that once again these were done in a batch, leaving the width of the parting tool in between each marked spacer. Once marked, part each spacer off. Remove the tailstock to enable the discs to come off. Sand each wheel and both sides of the spacers with an abrasive laid on a flat surface.

MODIFICATIONS AND CONSTRUCTION

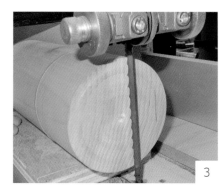

1 You need to mark where the cab will fit over the engine. You require a vertical cut on the engine to fix the cab against, and to determine how deep it will sit. I decided to cut lengthwise on the halfway mark.

2 The engine needs to be stable when it is cut. You could clamp it in a bench vise and hand-cut, but I used a bandsaw. For this, I created a right-angled cradle or sledge for the engine to sit in, so that I could clamp it securely in place and use the bandsaw to cut across the body to the required depth.

3 I then adjusted the position of the engine and cut lengthwise to meet the crosswise cut.

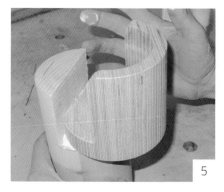

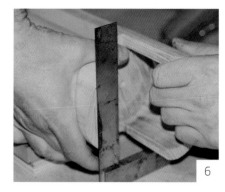

4 To get the cab to fit, you need to nip a bit off the bottom of the lower circle so that it will sit flat against the crosswise cut on the engine.

5 Sand the cab, and glue in place. You can see how this fits together. It leaves a very slight gap between the lower curve of the engine and the cab. Set aside to dry.

6 The engine needs to have a partial flat cut on the lower side to accept a rectangular section that will house the axles. It doesn't work to just fit them on the round body – this square section will make everything fit together well. Use the cradle or sledge once again to stabilize the piece. The cab will have to extend past the end of the sledge. The engine needs rotating to align the lower mark with the square.

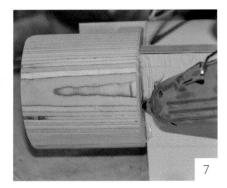

7 Use a combination of hot-melt glue and clamps (if they fit and don't get in the way) to hold everything stable.

8 Once everything is cured and set, use the bandsaw to cut lengthwise to the stop line, which is about 3 in. (75mm) from the nose of the engine. Once cut to that point, retract the blade from the cut and make a crosswise cut to depth, to sever the piece just cut.

9 You need to cut a rectangular section of wood, which will sit just wider than the flat just cut. Once created, drill the holes for the axles. Make the holes slightly oversize so the axles can turn. A drill press is ideal for this.

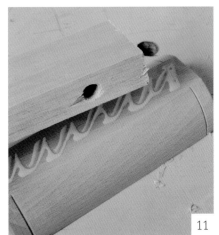

10 Once drilled and sanded, glue in place.

11 Cut or sand off a flat on the bottom of both carriages, to accept a full rectangular under-section running their length. Once the flats are in place on both carriages, and the rectangular underbody sections are cut, drilled and sanded, glue in place.

12 Clamps help keep the pressure on, and hold everything in place while the adhesive sets.

FINAL ASSEMBLY

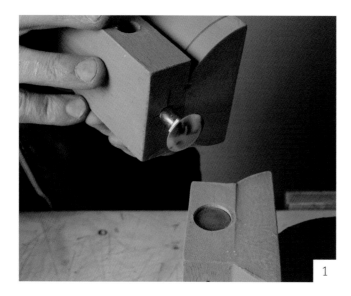

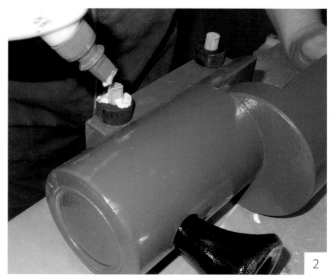

1 The carriages have to link together, and the engine needs to pull them along. Trial and error with rope and links worked, but this was ugly, so I decided to use ³/₄-in. by ¹/₈-in. (20 x 3mm) rare-earth magnets recessed in the front end of each carriage in the rectangular section. In the engine and the rear end of the first carriage, drill and glue in place a round-headed carriage bolt. Between the magnet and the bolt, there will be enough pull to keep the train and carriages together. Note that the pieces have had a coat of primer.

2 Paint or dye all the pieces in colors of your choice. Note the funnel in place on the engine. I must admit, I didn't photograph this when making it. The funnel is needed to make the steam engine look right. It is turned and glued in a drilled hole. The axles are cut to length and the spacers put in place. The spacers keep the inside edges of the wheels from touching the bodies of the engine and carriages. Thread the axles through the undercarriages, fit the spacers onto the axles and glue them in place. Keep the glue clear of the carriage body and where the axle touches the undercarriage as it needs to run smoothly, not be locked in place.

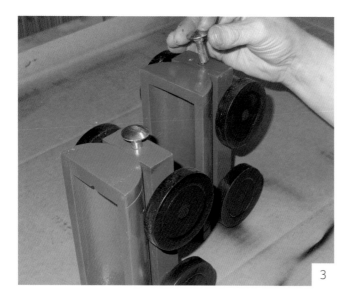

3 Glue the magnets in with epoxy resin and screw in the bolts. Glue the wheels to the spacers. Touch up any paintwork, then fit everything together.

Ring turning (also called hoop turning) is a method of mass-producing traditional wooden toys and ornaments. Typically, it employs end- or spindle-grain oriented turning using the ring section of a tree at least 10 in. (255mm) in diameter. The trick is to have the grain oriented to provide strength, and not short-grain sections where details can break off.

Ring-turned pigs

Here the ring is turned and shaped to represent the underside of an animal, then cut off to create a flat-topped ring with a hole in the center. The underside is jam-fitted onto a spigot on the trunk, which is held on the faceplate. You then shape the top to complete the form of the animal. The tricky bit is visualizing how the animal will look when in ring form. Once shaped, use a knife to slice from the outer area into the inner void (you will need to make two slices to remove the first animal from the ring).

I used spruce (*Picea* sp.) pieces from high in the Austrian Alps, the same wood as used by Austrian and German toymakers. Spruce is slow-growing due to the cold, making the growth rings close together. Fir and other slow-growing softwoods would also be suitable.

Expect to make mistakes and get the shapes wrong while you get the hang of this traditional turning method. But once you have mastered it, you will soon have a whole farmyard of animals.

Tools and materials

PPE: facemask/respirator

Drive spur, center and chuck

Faceplate

Sketching paper and pencils

Clear polycarbonate, ⅛ in. (3mm) thick

Bandsaw or handsaw

Rotary carving tool or coping saw

Abrasives, 120–400 grit

Screws, 2 in. (50mm)

Spindle roughing gouge

Spindle gouge

Bowl gouge

Thin parting tool

Beading and parting tool

Skew chisel

Parting tool, ³⁄₁₆ in. (5mm)

Paper towel

Carving knife

Large-bladed kitchen knife

Hammer

Protective gloves

Pull saw

Rotary carving tool with tapered burr

Toy-safe water-based paint and dye

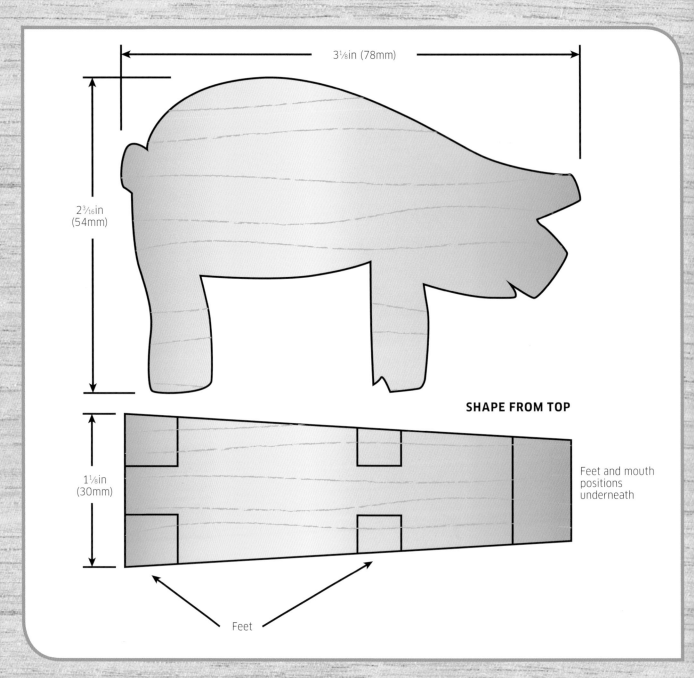

3⅛in (78mm)

2³⁄₁₆in
(54mm)

1⅛in
(30mm)

SHAPE FROM TOP

Feet and mouth
positions
underneath

Feet

The inspiration for this project came from the work produced in Seiffen, Germany, where ring- or hoop-turned animals have been made for hundreds of years.

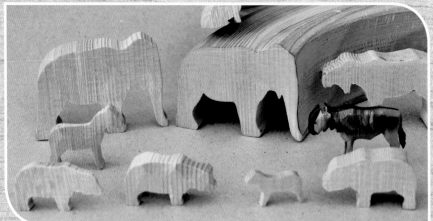

1

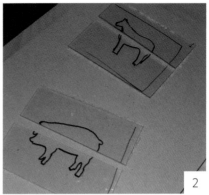

2

1 Sketch the animal shape. Don't overcomplicate the detail: you need a clearly defined outline easily identifiable as the animal. Keep the key characteristics and proportions in mind all the time. Lay ⅛-in. (3mm) thick clear polycarbonate over the top of your sketch, and trace the sketch on to it. This will be your template. Polycarbonate is ideal as it is shatterproof, but thin ply can also be used. Don't make the animals too small or too big. This one is just under 3½ in. (90mm) long and about 2¼ in. (55mm) high.

2 Cut the sheet into individual templates. I used a fine-toothed bandsaw, but a handsaw can also be used. Cut an oversized rectangle for each template, and then cut in half lengthwise. I used the pig, not the horse.

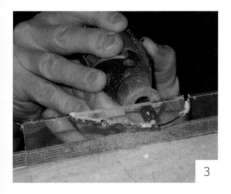

3

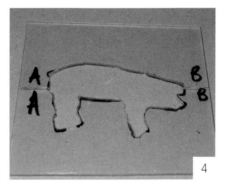

4

3 You need a template that you can lay against the work so that you can match the shape. Use either a rotary carving tool with a side-cut burr in it, or a coping saw, to remove the internal shape. When both halves are done, use abrasives to remove any anomalies and wispy bits.

4 There was too much detail in my first drawing, so I combined the leg sections into one block. Note also the nose and ear section. That V section is something easily turned, but there is no way I could feed the template into that detail, so this will be turned with the template removed. Note the A and B markings, so that I know which end is which. Note also that the saw cut to create the two halves of the template has squashed or flattened the form – see picture 2 – so I will have to allow for this in the turning.

Safety

Because the wood is large in diameter and possibly length, and often wet or certainly damp, make sure your lathe speeds are set lower than you would normally use for something of this diameter. Clean off the bark before you mount the work on a faceplate. Before starting up the lathe, check the rest position and rotate the wood by hand to make sure it clears the tool rest assembly.

5

6

5 Debark your tree ring – if you don't, there is a high likelihood of the bark coming off during turning. This log is just over 12 in. (300mm) long and 10 in. (255mm) wide but it could be shorter and narrower. A series of rings can be cut from this piece. If the rings created are quite narrow, you might get more than one ring across the width of the log.

It is best to start with a reasonable size, but if you are creating a farmyard then everything must be in proportion. Mount the log on a faceplate with six heavy-duty screws. Mount on the lathe with the tailstock and revolving center brought up to support the piece. Before switching on the lathe, rotate the work by hand to ensure nothing is in the way.

6 Keep the lathe speeds low and use a combination of spindle roughing gouge, spindle gouge and bowl gouge to create a smooth cylinder and to clean up the end grain.

7

8

9

7 The tailstock end of the wood will be the underside of the pig. Lay the template on the rest, but not touching the rotating wood, and use either pen or pencil to mark the main positions on the wood. You could also mark the tool rest with these positions, or use a thin parting tool to indent them.

8 Use the thin parting tool to incise the key positions with a plunge cut. The nose of the pig, near the center, has a wider cut to show the outer limit of the animal.

9 Once marked, use the thin parting tool or a beading and parting tool in conjunction with the spindle gouge to cut between the marks, creating the shapes required to fit the template. Try to cut with the grain where you can, but I must admit that I used a lot of plunge cuts with a parting tool at this stage. Nearer the finished profile, you need to make delicate cuts to avoid grain pull-out.

10 Stop regularly and check your cuts against the template. Note that the work should be stationary when this is done. You can see the sections that need to be cut away to make the template fit.

11 Use whichever tool you like to cut away the waste safely. Remember to minimize grain tear-out or you will have trouble later. A beading and parting tool is used here to refine and widen the recesses.

12 Check the cuts against the template. Note how the V section has been removed from the head end (B). This allows the template to slide in. The V can be cut onto the work later. At this stage, I needed to go deeper into the work.

13 Continue to make cuts with the most appropriate tool, working safely and minimizing tear-out. It can help with some cuts to use a skew in scraping mode, making a gentle cut.

14 The skew can also help when creating corners. A point tool would also work well for this, or a multi-tipped scraper fitted with a fine narrow tip of the right shape.

15 Continue to check against the template. You can see that it now fits. I used the corner of the skew to make an incised V cut to separate the area where the snout and ears will go. This is where the V section was taken off earlier near the letter B. Note the area where there is a clearly marked gap on the template.

16

17

16 When you are happy with the underside profile, measure and mark the height of the ring. The template shows what the body height will be. Remember to allow for the saw cut; I then allowed a bit more to trim off later.

17 Using a parting tool, make a plunge cut to a depth just greater than the height mark you have just placed on the outside of the log. Regularly retract the blade to clear the swarf, and make clearance cuts so that the blade does not bind. Large work requires thicker and longer blades for this. This parting tool is just about strong enough. Handle length and the amount of tang in the blade

all need checking to make sure everything is secure and safe. Specialist, heavy-duty straight (some are tapered) parting and coring bars can be used for this. Also, a multi-tipped scraper works well to open up a gap to width and depth here. The rule is to always work safe and be smart in your tool selection. If you have any doubts as to the suitability of a tool for a given job, don't use it.

18

19

20

18 Once the inner plunge cut is done, make the cut from the outer marked line. Again, use the safest tool and use the tailstock to provide support. Make clearance cuts and extract the blade regularly. Keep the lathe speed low, maybe 250–350 rpm.

19 Keep cutting until you meet the plunge cut made earlier in the center area. The tailstock prevents the ring rolling off, so keeping it nice and safe.

20 In this picture you can see the freed ring.

21 You now need to work on the top face of the ring to finish off the body shape. The ring is too large for a chuck to work, so the easiest method is to make a jam chuck by creating a spigot. The spigot can lock into the inner hole formed by the plunge cut in the center; or, as I chose, it can lock on to the front leg section near what will be the head of the pig. The bowl gouge or spindle gouge will create this spigot very quickly.

22 Here you can see where the spigot is cut and where it will fit into the ring section already turned. It needs to be a good fit that will not shift when shaping the top of the pig. When happy, tap it in place and check it is secure.

23 Lay the template against the work. Note that I have flipped the template over, so the head is still the end B nearest the tailstock. This was the shape I needed, but remember I had to allow for the thickness of the saw cut.

24 Use the tailstock to support the lower block. As long as it is not in the way it helps; and should the ring slip, the tailstock keeps it from falling on the floor. I started making cuts with a spindle gouge, but note the color change in the center of the ring. During the second shaping cut, the ring slipped a little, so I used two layers of paper towel to get a tight fit. There were no more problems after that. Using a combination of pull and push cuts with your spindle gouge, cutting with the grain, remove the waste and get to the preliminary shape required.

25 A delicate scrape with a skew in scraping mode cleaned up a few tiny bumps. Check the form against your template. Allowing for the difference in thickness, remove the ring and check it for thickness with calipers or your fingers. If you are not happy, relocate the ring and adjust until you are.

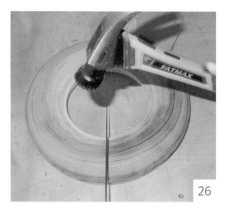

26 My pig was very slightly wedge-shaped; you might want a more even thickness along the body of your animal. Once shaped, remove the ring from the jam chuck and place it on a workbench or sturdy table. Sharpen an old kitchen carving knife, then lay it across the ring. With the knife blade held in the correct position, tap it hard. The ring should sever cleanly along the blade edge. This is a good reason for using straight-grained wood such as spruce.

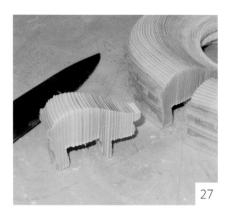

27 Although you have used a template, it is only when you have cut the first animal from the ring that you know whether or not the shape is right.

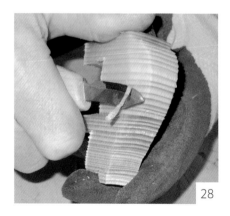

28 Now, you need to shape the pig fully. Traditionally, a knife is used for this. An anti-slash glove protects the hand holding the work and also the wrist. You could of course use a file or rasp, or a rotary carving tool with the appropriate bit, if you prefer.

29 Make multiple light cuts to create two ears. Then, shape the rest of the body. How much detail you add is up to you.

30 While holding the pig in a vise, I used a pull saw to remove the waste wood between its legs.

31 This picture shows a rotary carving tool with a burr fitted in it, cutting the waste wood between the legs. Note, however, how fluffy the cut wood is. This will need cleaning up with a knife and sanding.

32 It is up to you whether you color your work or not. I used a matte white, water-based paint, tinted with a touch of red concentrated dye to achieve a piggy pink. If all goes well, the result will be a nicely shaped pig in exactly the style you want.

Tea Party

Goodies such as cupcakes and muffins form the backbone of any tempting, sugar-laden tea party. They can be created in myriad designs, with the tops worked to represent all sorts of shapes and toppings, to make an attractive display of teatime treats.

Cupcakes and muffins

Tools and materials

PPE: facemask/respirator

Drive spur and revolving center

Chuck

Spindle roughing gouge

Spindle gouge

Beading and parting tool

Thin parting tool

Bead forming tool

Skew, scraper or gouge

Abrasives, 120–400 grit

Drill and sanding arbor, or disc sander

Toy-safe dye

Toy-safe lacquer

Finish and colors of your choice

This is a spindle-grain project. Your first decision is what sort of wood to use. I chose to use maple because it is light in color and takes dye well. Other light woods that work are sycamore (*Acer pseudoplatanus*), beech (*Fagus* spp.) and fruitwoods. One wood that works very well if you want to make chocolate cakes is walnut (*Juglans* spp.). Its deep, rich, brown color is excellent for the bases, but if you want colored frosting and such on top you will have to use paints rather than dyes. All the woods mentioned take fine detail and carve easily too.

Your second decision is whether to make solid cakes, or slightly more complicated ones that can be cut open over and over again. If you wish to create cakes that can be cut open, you need to decide where the join for the two parts will be. This will have a bearing on your joining options, which might be anything from a spigot and recess, magnet, or hook-and-loop fixing to link the parts. If using magnets or hook-and-loop fixings, make sure your adhesive secures everything in place properly and that it has no way of coming loose, otherwise the small parts will be a choking hazard.

Safety warning

Make sure you use finishes that are suitable for children. Dyes and lacquers should be clearly marked as toy-safe in case these little cakes end up in a child's mouth.

MUFFIN

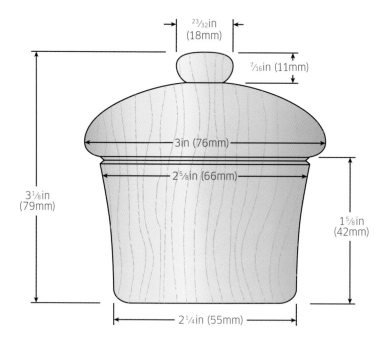

$^{23}/_{32}$in (18mm)

$^7/_{16}$in (11mm)

3in (76mm)

2$^5/_8$in (66mm)

3$^1/_8$in (79mm)

1$^5/_8$in (42mm)

2$^1/_4$in (55mm)

CUPCAKE

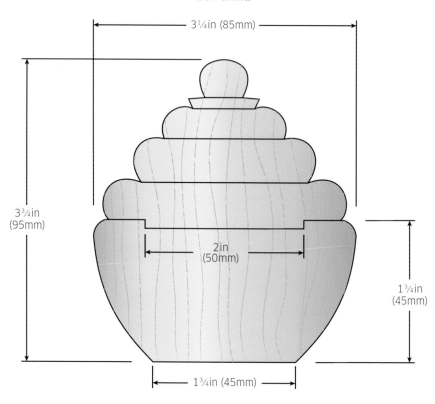

3$^1/_4$in (85mm)

3$^3/_4$in (95mm)

2in (50mm)

1$^3/_4$in (45mm)

1$^3/_4$in (45mm)

1 Mount the wood between centers, and use a spindle roughing gouge to turn to size. Cut a spigot at one end with a beading/parting tool, then mount in the chuck. I wanted to create a solid, simple cake with some sort of ball-type top on it. This could represent a bobble of frosting or something like a jelly sweet or cherry. You can decide on this when it comes to coloring.

2 Make multiple light cuts to minimize damage and made sure you get your intended shape right with no flat spots. Remember, with spindle-grain projects you should try to cut downhill with the grain to ensure the best possible cuts.

3 I wanted the top of the cake to look as though it had some form of frosting on it, and the top section to look as though it had popped over the top of the bun tray. The piece is wider at the top than on the main body, so rounding over the outer lower section of the top needed to be done before the shaping of the lower body area.

4 When you have set the maximum width of the top, continue with the rolled section so that you roll over until you reach the top section of the body of the cupcake.

5 You can see now how smooth the top is, and how the rolled lower section of the top and the body meet. There is a slight V-shaped groove between the two, which will help with the coloring later.

6 The body should have a slight taper to it. Most cake tins have this, and you can easily copy that detail.

7 Continue to refine the shape until you are happy.

8 Use a parting tool to cut partway through the bottom end of the body. You now know the depth. Make sure it looks visually balanced.

9

10

9 The outer edge of the piece has a slight chamfer. You can angle the parting tool or use a skew, scraper or gouge for this. If you are having trouble getting the shape you want with a gouge, remember that a suitably shaped scraper or skew can be used to scrape a surface.

10 Sand the piece all over.

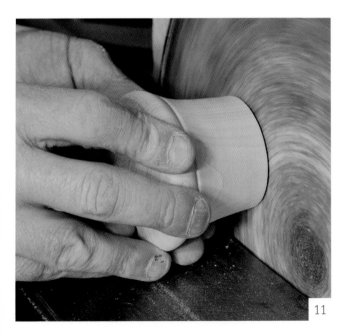

11

12

11 Part or cut off the cake from the waste and sand the bottom. You can do this either by hand, by using a drill and sanding arbor, or on a disc sander if you prefer.

12 Color the cakes to finish. I used several different-colored dyes, followed by a coat of lacquer to seal them.

Additions

You can carve or enhance the base section further, if you wish. Using a rotary carving tool and a drum sander will enable you to cut flute-like details easily. Work the lower part first, then work the upper half to meet it. The base shown here will have a top that is joined to it via a magnet. If you don't want to use a hook-and-loop or magnet fixing, create a spigot fit between the top and the base.

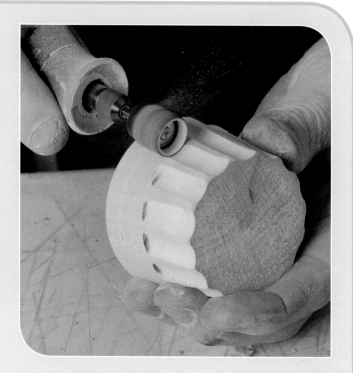

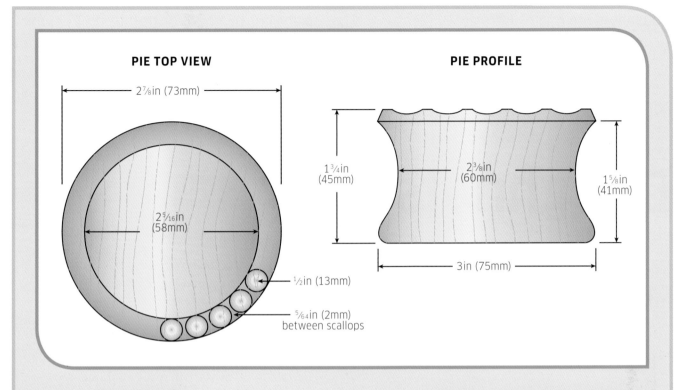

PIE TOP VIEW

2⅞in (73mm)

2⁵⁄₁₆in (58mm)

½in (13mm)

⁵⁄₆₄in (2mm) between scallops

PIE PROFILE

1¾in (45mm)

2⅜in (60mm)

1⅝in (41mm)

3in (75mm)

Variation: Pies

Pies are simple to make as a variation on the muffin and cupcake designs. Again, you need to decide if you want to be able to cut the piece open; and, if so, whether you wish to use magnets, or a hook-and-loop, or spigot and recess, fixing. I would suggest using hook-and-loop fixings or magnets, because a push fitting doesn't work particularly well here. For decoration, you could leave the pastry crust plain or decorate it with some carved or textured detail. The inner section, when open, can have a two-tone color system to convey the crust and filling.

Two pies: one left whole but with a fluted edge and one left plain but cut in half, with the inside colored to represent the pie filling and crust.

Doughnuts are one of life's guilty pleasures. They might not be good for us, but they are so delicious that it would be remiss not to include them in a tea-party line-up. It's a good idea to have a few real ones around for reference while you're working, but I have to confess that I ate mine before I finished the project!

Doughnuts

Tools and materials

PPE: facemask/respirator

Drive spur and revolving center

Chuck

Bowl gouge

Angled scraper or skew chisel

Abrasives, 120–400 grit

Parting tool

Handsaw

Hot-melt glue gun

Thin parting tool

Cordless drill and ½-in. (13mm) drum sander

Toy-safe dye

Satin lacquer

Thinned gloss paint

Drill chuck with ⅝–¾-in. (15–20mm) drill bit

Turned doughnuts can be made from spindle-grain or bowl/faceplate-grain oriented wood. Whichever grain orientation you opt for, there will be short grain somewhere – so be sure to make the doughnuts large enough not to break across that short grain. I used bowl/faceplate-grain oriented sycamore (*Acer pseudoplatanus*) as you can readily obtain large diameters. Getting 4-in. (100mm) diameter spindle-grain oriented wood can be tricky. You could, of course, glue up laminated birch-faced ply to the size you require.

There are two methods for making doughnuts, which differ according to how you create the all-important hole in the middle. I used the hot-glue chuck method, which I find is easier and gives more freedom shape-wise. For this, you wholly turn the piece before using a hot-glue chuck to hold the turned upper side while you finish off your doughnut form.

The second method is to start by drilling a hole all the way through, then to use a jam-chuck to hold the drilled ring while you finish the shape. Alongside the hot-glue chuck method, I will show you the key parts for the drilled hole and jam-chuck technique.

TOP VIEW

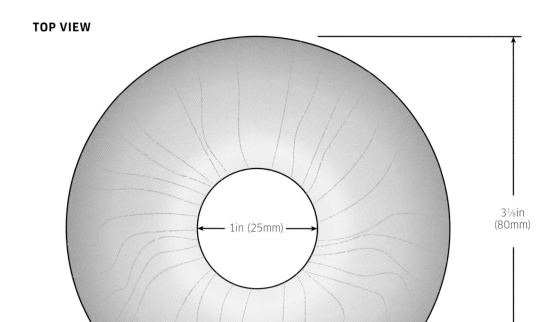

1in (25mm)

3⅛in
(80mm)

SIDE VIEW

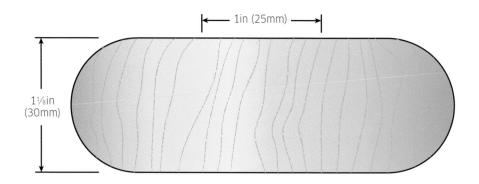

1in (25mm)

1⅛in
(30mm)

1 Create a cylinder of wood between centers. I used bowl/faceplate-grain oriented sycamore for this project, so I used a bowl gouge and worked the wood as I would when cutting a bowl. If you use spindle-grain oriented wood, use a spindle roughing gouge and spindle gouge and cut as you would any other spindle work. Cut a spigot at one end to fit your chuck.

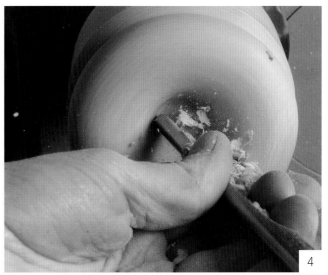

2 Start to shape the curved top of the doughnut. Note that the flute of the gouge points in the direction of the cut, and the cut occurs on the lower wing. You can see the inner hollow started here. Continue until you get close to the center, so that you have an idea of the shape.

3 I used the bowl gouge to start cutting the back by beginning to create the outer edge profile, which was effectively a large bead.

4 Once I had formed the outer shape and depth of the doughnut, I went back to the middle section and formed one side of the gently sloping hole.

5 I often use a scraper to refine cut surfaces, because it results in a smoother, more refined shape that is easier to sand due to lack of bumps and unevenness. I use an angled scraper to do this, but if you do not have one then a skew chisel laid on its side works very well.

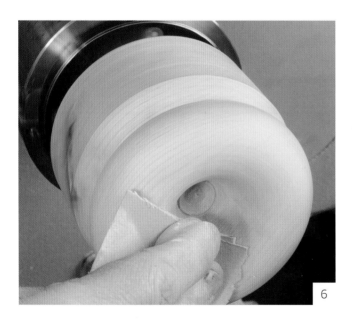

6 Once you have the outer and inner shape as you want it, sand down to about 320–400 grit.

7 Use a parting tool to part off the shaped doughnut, making sure you part off enough so that you can achieve the shape you need. Part most of the way through. I didn't want the piece to fall on the ground and be damaged, so I stopped the lathe and used a handsaw to cut though the last little bit.

8 Take a section of waste wood and create a sloping taper that resembles (and can cradle centrally) the top face of the doughnut. When you are happy with the shape and fit, apply a small amount of hot-melt glue, just enough to hold the doughnut securely. Don't worry about the glue marking the surface; it rubs off easily later on. You could use industrial double-sided carpet tape for this job instead.

Tip Note that when you make items such as wheels for other toys, you use methods similar to the two shown for this project.

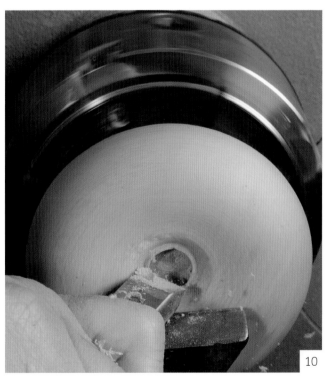

9 The doughnut needs placing on the glue and centralizing quickly. I used the tailstock to help with this, keeping it in place for as long as possible while shaping, and only removing it when I needed to reach the inner section. Use the bowl gouge to make successive shaping cuts, creating the outer and top profiles before eventually reaching into the center area.

10 When you are ready, remove the tailstock and shape the inner section. Again, use the angled scraper or skew chisel to clean up after the gouge work is done. When you are ready, sand the doughnut.

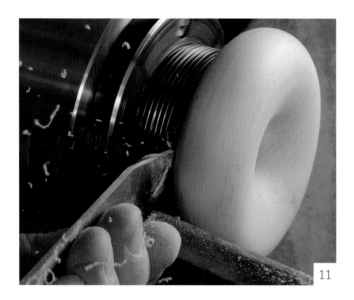

11 Use a parting tool – a thin one in this case – to remove some of the waste-wood chuck at the back. Remember not to touch the shaped doughnut section, and be careful not to touch the jaws with the blade. In the photograph, it looks as though the blade is close to the jaws, but in reality it is over ¼ in. (6mm) away. With the lathe stopped, you might be able to push the piece off, but this could indicate a weaker hold than I like to use.

12 Now, with the lathe stopped, and having removed some of the waste (and thereby some of the glue holding the piece), you can push the doughnut off the glue chuck. If you can't do this the first time, remove more wood from the waste-wood chuck until you can.

13 Use a drill fitted with a drum sander to clean up the inside of the hole. Alternatively, you could use a round file or a rod with abrasive wrapped round it.

14 Color your doughnut. I used a brush to apply a light dye, followed by a coat of satin lacquer. You could also lay a color glaze on top, using a thinned gloss paint to represent the sugar glaze found on some doughnuts.

Alternative method

1 Mount your cylinder of wood in the lathe, and drill a hole in the center to your chosen size using a drill chuck with appropriate-sized bit. Then, shape the outside and the exposed top section of the doughnut. Once shaped as far as you can, sand it and then part it off and repeat the process to create many part-turned doughnuts. Once done, mount a waste-wood offcut of wood in your chuck. Create a spigot just larger than the diameter of the hole drilled in the doughnut. Place the turned face onto the wooden spigot and test for fit. Adjust as required to get a nice tight fit when the doughnut is placed on it.

2 Fit the doughnut to the spigot. If the fit is a little slack, wrap paper towel around the spigot before sliding on the doughnut to get everything snug and secure. You need a good fit because you will be cutting the new exposed top face and part of the rest of the side of the doughnut. If you have any doubts about the security of the doughnut, take some duct tape or similar and wrap it around the lower, finished section of the doughnut and around the exposed section of the waste-wood chuck. You now have an extra bit of security to keep everything in place. Start up the lathe at a lowish speed, and then begin to shape the rest of the doughnut

3 Shape the piece to get a nice even shape and then sand it. You will end up with a small, flat area in the hole where it is held on the waste-wood spigot. This will need blending in with the drum sander once it is freed from the jam chuck.

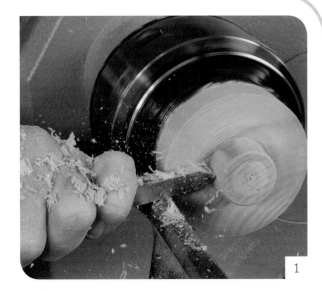

A large cake will form the show-stopping centerpiece of the tea party. I based this cake design on a Victoria sandwich, with a generous filling of cream and jam, and a top dusted with confectioners sugar. That is the beauty of this type of work: you can create whatever you wish.

Sponge cake

Tools and materials

PPE: facemask/respirator

Drive spur and revolving center

Chuck/faceplate

Bowl gouge

Abrasives, 120–400 grit

Bead forming tool, ½–⅝ in. (13–16mm)

Thin parting tool

Bead forming tool, ⅛ in. (3mm)

Indexing system or ruler

Bandsaw or handsaw

Disc sander, or strip of abrasive on a bench or length of board

Toy-safe dye, light brown

Primer, white

Toy-safe pen, red

Magnets

Drill

Epoxy glue

Friction drive with rubber shield

This is a simple project that uses a bowl/faceplate-grain oriented blank. I used boxelder (*Acer negundo*), but sycamore (*Acer pseudoplatanus*), beech (*Fagus* spp.) and other close-grained hardwoods will work as well.

Boxelder often has lovely red and brown coloration running through it. If this is strong enough visually, there is no need to apply the additional dye – just leave the wood in its natural state for the main body and create a color on top to represent the dusting, frosting or iced topping

I decided not to turn any small candles, sweets or decorations for the top. You could add these, but remember that small parts represent choke hazards. If you make small pieces that look like delicious sweets, they might get mistaken for the real thing.

Tip You don't have to use magnets to hold this piece together. It works well as loose sections, but using magnets makes it more fun to cut the cake.

SIDE PROFILE

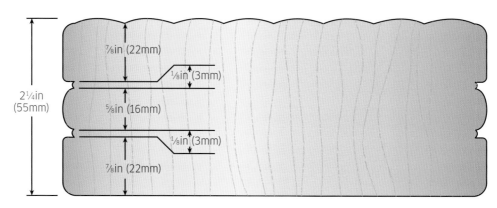

7⁄8in (22mm)

1⁄8in (3mm)

2¼in (55mm)

5⁄8in (16mm)

1⁄8in (3mm)

7⁄8in (22mm)

TOP VIEW

Ø = overall diameter

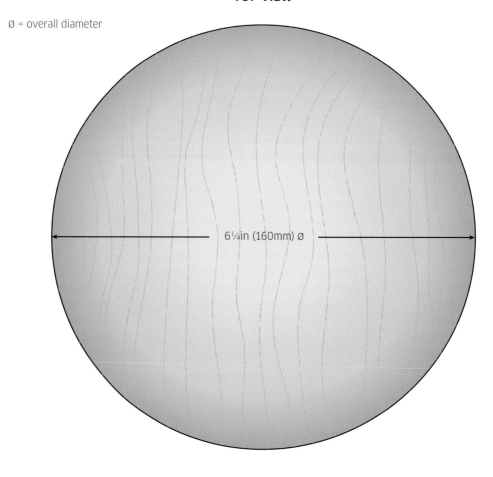

6¼in (160mm) Ø

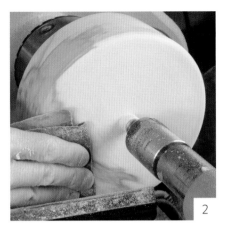

1 Find the centers of both faces and mount between centers. Use a bowl gouge to clean up the tailstock end, as this will become the base for the cake.

2 Once the tailstock end is clean, sand it. Note the small nub that is left under the tailstock ring center. This will be used to locate the drive center perfectly in the next step.

3 When you have finished sanding, remove the blank from the lathe and reverse it. You will have the location mark of the ring or revolving center to locate the drive, and the drive center mark to locate the tailstock center. Use the bowl gouge to clean up the face.

Tip Instead of mounting the blank between centers, you could mount it on a small screw chuck, as the central hole will be where the cake is sawn so won't show.

4 Refine the edge, as required. I used a bowl gouge but a scraper might be suitable too, depending on the wood.

5 Use a large bead forming tool to cut the central bead that represents a cream filling. Alternatively, you can use a gouge followed by a skew, or a point tool in scraping mode, to cut this main central bead.

6 Either side of the large central bead, you need two smaller beads to represent jam fillings. I started by using a thin parting tool to recess either side of the main bead, to the depth I required for the crowns of the small beads.

7

7 Then, I used a small ⅛-in. (3mm) bead forming tool to cut the beads. These small beads are recessed quite a way into the wood, so they are tricky to do without using a forming tool. You can make or buy one, or perhaps use a combination of a thin parting tool and a point tool to cut the bead form. Alternatively, just leave it square from the parting tool.

8

8 The effect of the beads is of a bulging sandwich of jam, cream and more jam.

9

9 Use the gouge to create some form of texture or detail on the top of the cake. Undulating, bead-like forms in different sizes worked well for me.

10

10 Sand the top and the outer edge to a fine finish.

11

11 Remove the piece from the lathe. Chisel off the nubs on the bottom and top, then sand the rough areas.

12

12 Mount the piece between centers once more, using a friction drive with non-marring heads. Note the rubber shield on the revolving center. Use an indexing system to mark the cake segments, or judge them by eye and mark with a ruler.

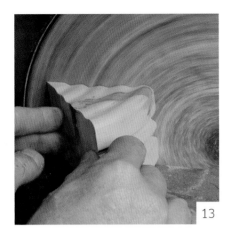

13

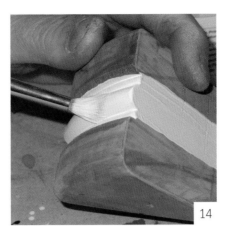

14

15

13 Bandsaw the sections, or cut them by hand while the cake is held in a non-marring vise. You can leave the bandsaw marks to imitate the marks of knife on cake, or sand everything smooth using a disk sander or a strip of abrasive on a bench. I chose to sand the pieces.

14 Stain the wood with light-colored dye to represent the color of the sponge cake. Use a white primer on the central bead, for the cream that sandwiches the two halves of the cake together.

15 Color the outer beads a vibrant red, to represent the jam. I used a pen, but had to cut the tip into a chisel shape to reach the depth of the smaller beads. In hindsight, a brush and paint might have worked better.

16

16 You can leave the cake slices loose, or link them so that they can appear to be cut apart. Magnets or hook-and-loop fixings will both work well. I used magnets, drilling holes for them and gluing in place with epoxy. After fixing, a quick sand and a touch-up of color disguises everything nicely.

These meringue-based cakes are typically made in bright, eye-catching colors. Macarons will be a very popular addition to the turned tea party because of their visual appeal, and they can be made quite easily from spindle-grain or faceplate-grain oriented wood. I have opted for chocolate fillings throughout but you could match to the outside colors.

Macarons

Tools and materials

PPE: facemask/respirator

Drive spur and revolving center

Chuck

Spindle roughing gouge

Spindle gouge

Bead forming tool

Angled scraper or skew chisel

Beading and parting tool

Thin parting tool

Abrasives, 120–400 grit

Drill and sanding arbor

Toy-safe pens in assorted colors

Toy-safe dye and small paintbrush

Toy-safe lacquer

I chose spindle-grain / endgrain oriented ash (*Fraxinus* spp.) and maple (*Acer* spp.) to make my macarons. Ash has a more pronounced and open grain than that of maple, creating a lovely look when colored. The coloring highlighted the grain due to differential color absorption. The maple gives a nice, more even look to the macaron.

The outsides were colored with toy-safe pens, and I then used a small paintbrush to apply toy-safe dye to color the inner section so it looked like a chocolate ganache filling. To finish, I sprayed the macarons with toy-safe lacquer to fix the colors.

The technique for making burgers is similar to that used for the macarons. I know burgers are not usually part of a tea party, but kids love them and they are much easier to turn than sandwiches!

Tip If you go along to the local baker, patisserie or cake specialist you will see plenty of wonderful goodies to provide inspiration for a selection of delicious cakes and sweet treats for your tea party mix.

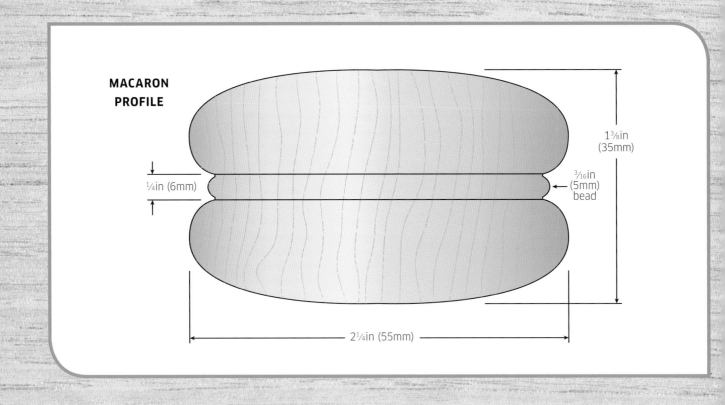

MACARON PROFILE

1³⁄₈in (35mm)

¼in (6mm)

³⁄₁₆in (5mm) bead

2¼in (55mm)

1

2

3

1 Mount the wood between centers, and use a spindle roughing gouge to turn to size. Cut a spigot at one end with a beading and parting tool, then mount in the chuck and use a spindle gouge to create a flattened dome shape for the top half of the macaron.

2 Once the top half is cut, use the spindle gouge to start shaping the back section of the macaron. Don't make it too thin at this stage, or you will not be able to finish off the shaping and detail to the level required.

3 You can see that the underside is shaped to match the top, and the middle has a band around it. This is where you will add the detail to represent the filling.

4 Using the spindle gouge, work the middle band and start to define the rolled-over inner edges of the top and bottom sections.

5 Make sure that you cut a fair way in, so that the 'filling' is inside the outer edges of the top and bottom sections.

6 You want a bead in this area. A small $^3/_{16}$-in. (5mm) bead is ideal: you can use the gouge to create this.

7 Alternatively, you can use a bead forming tool.

8 Refine the rolled-over sections that meet the bead you have cut. A gouge, angled scraper or skew chisel will work here.

9 Once cut, use a parting tool to refine the lower section. A thin parting tool works in this confined area better than a gouge. Be careful not to part all the way through.

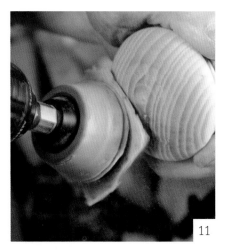

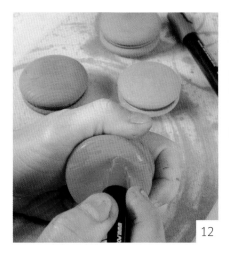

10 Leave sufficient thickness so that you can sand almost all the available surfaces.

11 When you have finished sanding, cut off the piece from the waste and sand the bottom section. A drill with sanding arbor is ideal for this.

12 Color the macarons as you wish. The outer sections are the brightly colored areas, for which I used toy-safe pens.

13 Usually, the macaron filling is either brown or white, or matches the outsides, but in this case I made them all brown (chocolate).

I used a toy-safe dye that could be applied with a brush, as toy-safe pens would not reach into the confined area of the inner bead.

14 Once the macarons have been colored, give them a coating of lacquer to fix.

Variation: Burger

1 To make a burger, you require a loose inner section for the patty, with a separate top and bottom for the bun. You can cut the bun sections easily.

2 The inner patty section is just a disc which can, if you choose, have some texture applied to it with a texturing or knurling tool. I only do that on one face and the edges. That said, you can reverse the piece and hold it with strong double-sided tape, on a vacuum chuck, in a jam chuck or in Cole jaws and texture the other side.

3 The finish is two types of dye, which are sealed with lacquer.

My grandmother made delicious jam tarts when I was young, with wonderful pastry and jam fillings of different flavors and colors, so I felt these were an essential tea party treat. Jam tarts are very easy to make, and I dyed the 'pastry' sections of the turned tarts and used different-colored toy-safe pens to recreate the tarts I remember so fondly.

Jam tarts

Tools and materials

PPE: facemask/respirator

Drive spur and revolving center

Chuck

Spindle roughing gouge

Spindle gouge

Angled scraper or skew chisel

Beading and parting tool

Texturing tool or spiraling tool, optional

Abrasives, 120–400 grit

Thin parting tool

Brushes

Toy-safe dye

Toy-safe pens

Toy-safe lacquer

I decided to make the jam tarts as a spindle-grain turning project. Whichever wood you use, whether spindle and/or faceplate-grain oriented, there will be short grain somewhere. So, do not make the jam tarts too thin because they will then be at risk of becoming bent or twisted during play. This twisting and bending might cause a break across the grain, which would make the toy unsafe for young children.

I tested various woods and decided upon sycamore, a maple (*Acer* spp.), with beech (*Fagus* sp.) coming a close second option. I found that the combination of a thick base section with a raised side-wall to create the rim made for an item that is both stable and fit for purpose.

Of course, you should try things out for yourself to make sure you are happy, but here is how I made my turned jam tarts.

Tip I decided to create some texture in the middle section of the tarts, which in real jam tarts would be where the jam is. This texture absorbs the color applied to various degrees and adds a little extra to the design. I found the plain, untextured surfaces in my early attempts to be bland and not as attractive.

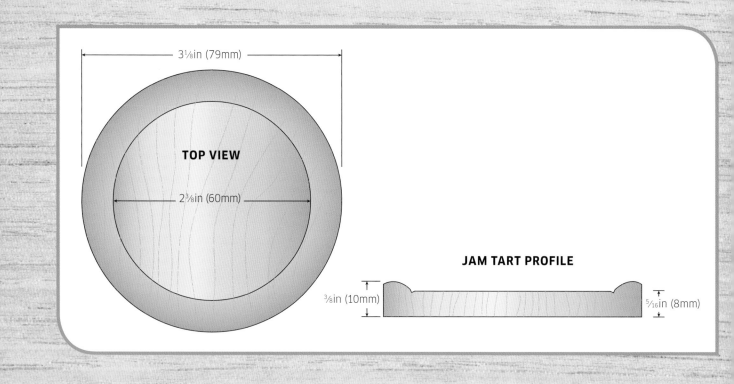

TOP VIEW

3⅛in (79mm)

2⅜in (60mm)

JAM TART PROFILE

⅜in (10mm)

⁵⁄₁₆in (8mm)

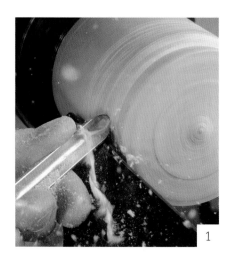

1

2

3

1 Mount your spindle-grain oriented wood between centers. Create a smooth cylinder with the spindle roughing gouge. Cut a spigot with a beading and parting tool. Remove the wood from the lathe and mount the spigot in the chuck jaws.

2 Use a spindle gouge to shape the outside of the jam tart. The wall can be square or sloping towards the base. Round over the rim of what represents the pastry.

3 Once the rim is cut, use the standard hollowing pull cut – where the gouge flute points at about the 10 o'clock position as viewed on a clock face. Work from the center towards the outer edge, with the cut occurring on the lower wing of the gouge. Stop just shy of the required wall thickness and make a second cut if you need it to get to the depth required.

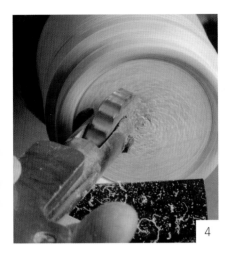

4

5

6

4 Clean up the inner surface. I used an angled scraper/ skew on its side in scraping mode and then opted to use a spiraling and texturing tool to create a few dimples and slight swirls in the center area. The cutter was just off vertical and pulled from the center out to the rim. A few passes were required to get the detail I needed. You could also use this tool or a rotary carving tool to create some texture on the pastry rim.

5 When you are happy with the texturing pattern, you are ready to sand the piece. Sand lightly with a fine grit grade on the textured inner section, to avoid removing the pattern.

6 After sanding, I noticed a small defect so I refined the outer section a little. Don't be afraid to do this if required. A light re-sand cleaned the piece up after the cut.

8

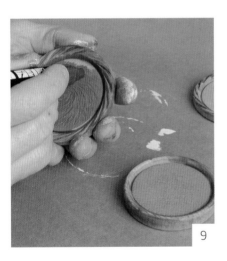

9

7

7 Use a thin parting tool to part almost all the way through.

8 Cut the piece free with the parting tool. As it is such a small item, I supported it with my hand. If you do this, take extra care that all body parts, clothing, jewelry and items that could get caught are kept well clear of any revolving parts of the lathe.

9 Sand the base, and color your tarts in the desired flavors and then give them a coat of matte or satin lacquer or similar to seal everything in. If you fancy doing something a bit different, apply a gloss layer to the inner section to make it look more like real jam.

An irresistible treat for adults and children alike, ice cream is a very welcome addition on the menu at a children's tea party. With ice cream, the flavor options (and, therefore, the coloring options for your project) seem almost infinite. To make these turned ice cream cones I used a maple species, but any close-grained hardwood should work.

Ice cream cones

Tools and materials

PPE: facemask/respirator

Drive spur and revolving center

Chuck

Spindle roughing gouge

Spindle gouge

Thin parting tool

Beading and parting tool

Spiraling tool or other texturing tool

Angled scraper or skew chisel

Abrasives, 120–400 grit

Toy-safe dye

Brushes

Primer

Toy-safe lacquer

Gloss paint

This is a spindle-grain oriented project. It is a simple piece of work, which you can make more complex by adding some form of texture to the ice cream cone. That is optional, but it does give you some scope for personalizing things and making the project feel very much your own.

I made this in one piece, but like the cupcakes you can make the ice cream part removable from the main body. The cone has a rounded end and thickens as the main body shape sweeps up to the ice cream. Make the cone too thin and it is a choke hazard.

I used European sycamore (*Acer pseudoplatanus*), but as mentioned elsewhere in the book, many other woods can be used instead. I chose a maple species because it will hold detail and texture well. Softer woods are more problematic.

I have chosen to show the basic ice cream with the scoop of ice cream on top in the dimensioned drawing, but show how to add the beaded ice cream and spiraled cone in the step-by-step guide.

Tip I made a one-piece ice cream cone with a scoop of ice cream which was then colored. You could make this in two parts and use a light biscuit-colored wood for the cone and a contrasting wood for the scoop of ice cream. Walnut (*Juglans* spp.) would be an ideal wood to represent chocolate ice cream. Experiment and find what you like. To join the two parts, you can use a hook-and-loop fastener.

ICE CREAM PROFILE

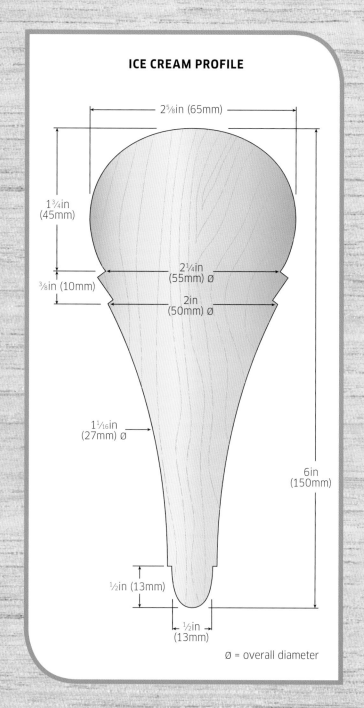

2⅝in (65mm)

1¾in (45mm)

⅜in (10mm)

2¼in (55mm) Ø

2in (50mm) Ø

1¹⁄₁₆in (27mm) Ø

6in (150mm)

½in (13mm)

½in (13mm)

Ø = overall diameter

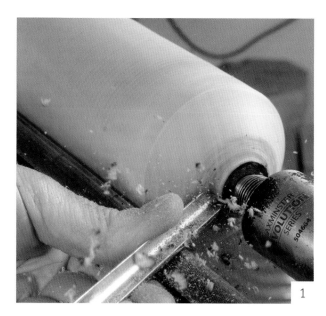

1

1 Mount your spindle-grain oriented wood between centers. Create a smooth cylinder with the spindle roughing gouge. Cut a spigot using a beading and parting tool. Remove the wood from the lathe and mount the spigot in the chuck jaws. Then, bring up the tailstock to support the free end. Using a spindle gouge, begin to shape the scoop of ice cream that will sit on the cone.

2

2 Use the spindle gouge to start to refine the stem. Block in the top quarter section.

3 Move back to the top section of the ice cream and cut a series of bead-like sections. You can also, if you choose, cut something that resembles either the shape of a scoop of ice cream or, as shown here, the swirled shape formed by an ice cream dispenser.

4 Refine the shapes as you go along and don't be afraid to tinker with the cut profiles. Remember, always cut with the grain. In this case, on a spindle-grain project, we are cutting from the largest section down to the smallest to ensure clean cuts. Having shaped the main part of the ice cream, remove the tailstock support so that you can access the very tip.

5 Start to refine the cone section. Remove some of the waste, and refine the shape as you go.

6 Cut in gentle stages to ensure that you do not apply too much pressure to the cone.

7 Depending on the length of your wood, and how thin you go, you might find that you need to support the ice cream end with the tailstock again. If you do this, you can use a rubber bung to prevent marking the top with the revolving center.

8 You can see that almost all of the cone is now shaped. Aesthetically, it's a very pleasing shape, but it can be a little bland without some form of decoration.

9 Add decoration to the cone, if desired. I used a spiraling tool to cut a spiral down most of the cone. If you do this, you must maintain pressure into the work so that the cutter remains in the cut grooves. Otherwise, you will end up cutting a new spiral. The trick is to cut your initial spiral to about $5/_{32}$ in. (4mm) deep, then remove the tool. Always cut in the direction the cutter is tilted, and cut with the grain.

10 Relocate the tool at the starting point, with the blade horizontal, before tilting down to get the cutter to cut once more. The pitch of the spiral changes as the diameter reduces, so you can only get about two-thirds of the way with this $1/_4$-in. (6mm) cutter.

11 A different type of pattern can be achieved by holding the cutter perpendicular, to create a knurled (finely ridged) effect.

12 Sand the piece to a fine finish, angling the abrasive to clean the inner spiral section a little. When you have finished, cut through the lower end of the cone and sand this to a nice, rounded form.

13 Apply your choice of color and finish. I made two ice cream cones. One has a knurled cone with a plain scoop of ice cream. The other has a spiral decoration on the cone with a swirled ice cream topping. I dyed the cones a light biscuit color and then used a primer for the ice cream before spraying on a lacquer to seal the dye.

14 Finally, I applied a coat of gloss paint to the ice cream to make it look more realistic.

A knife is a necessary item at any tea party, to cut the various delicacies on offer. Some of the projects in our turned toys tea party are joined by hook-and-loop tape or magnets, and this little wooden knife is ideal for separating them.

Knife

Tools and materials

PPE: facemask/respirator

Drive spur and revolving center

Chuck

Thin parting tool

Spindle roughing gouge

Spindle gouge

Skew chisel

Bead forming tool, ³⁄₁₆ in. (5mm)

Abrasives, down to 320 grit

Bandsaw or handsaw

Disc sander

Finish and colors of your choice

The process for creating a knife is very similar to that for creating a spatula or other cooking utensil. It does, however, require you to do some shaping of the blade. I chose to sand it to shape on a disc sander, but if you prefer you can use a knife to whittle it. Sycamore and maple (*Acer* spp.), beech (*Fagus* spp.), birch (*Betula* spp.), walnut (*Juglans* spp.), and fruitwoods would be ideal for this project.

Be careful when designing knives, spoons and other utensils. They are thin so can be a choking hazard. Depending on the handle shape, they can also be prone to breaking if this area or the joins between the blade and handle are put under too much stress.

Safety warning

So that this toy is safe for children to use, make sure there are no sharp edges when you shape the blade. If you round off the edges this will stop the wood from breaking or splintering.

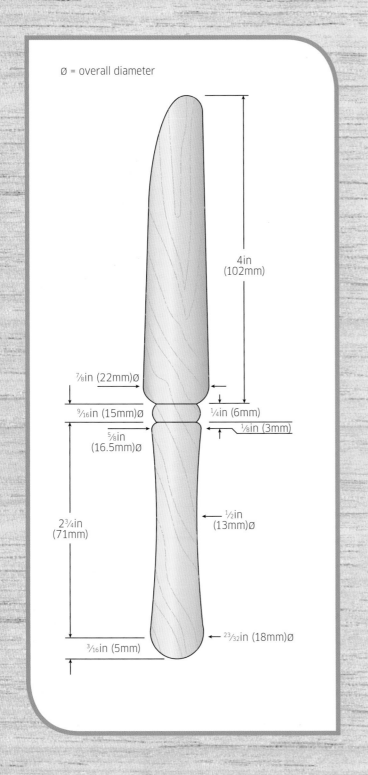

Ø = overall diameter

4in
(102mm)

⁷⁄₈in (22mm)Ø

⁹⁄₁₆in (15mm)Ø

¼in (6mm)

⅛in (3mm)

⁵⁄₈in
(16.5mm)Ø

2¾in
(71mm)

½in
(13mm)Ø

³⁄₁₆in (5mm)

²³⁄₃₂in (18mm)Ø

1 I decided to use a square section of wood. Hold the end which will become the blade end of the knife in the chuck. Support what will become the handle end of the knife with a revolving ring center. A thin parting tool is ideal for marking the transition point between the end of the handle and the start of the blade.

2 Make the cut just deep enough to part down through the square corners to the solid section.

3

3 Use a spindle roughing gouge to smooth down the handle section. Note how the flute points in the direction of the cut, and the cut is on the lower wing. The wing should be at the 9 o'clock position when it meets the cut shoulder, so there is no risk of a catch.

4

5

4 Use a spindle gouge to shape the handle. It will need to be sturdy enough to use to separate the sections of sponge cake, so don't make it too thin. An elongated cove form will work well. The end can just be dome-shaped.

5 You can see the square shoulder created by the parting tool – this will eventually be a bead. Shape the handle with this in mind.

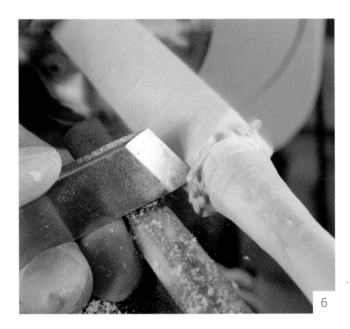

6 A skew chisel can be used to create a gentle arc for the bottom section of the blade.

7 Add a bead at the transition point between the handle and blade. A $^3/_{16}$-in. (5mm) bead forming tool was used here, but you can also roll the bead using a gouge or a skew point. It is small, though, so the forming tool works well.

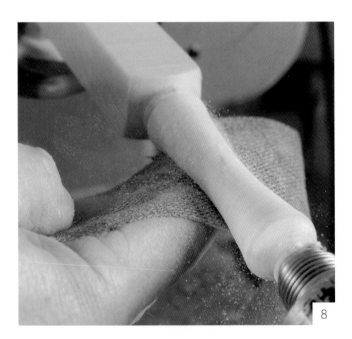

8 When you have finished cutting the bead, sand the handle to a fine grit grade.

9 Now the handle is shaped and sanded, remove the tailstock and refine the end of the handle. A light cut with the skew is ideal. Sand the end.

10

10 To minimize excess sanding, I removed some of the waste on the blade section with a bandsaw (if you don't want to do this, you can just sand or carve the blade more). No fingers are in the line of cut of the blade; and, being flat, the piece is stable during the cut. I stopped short of the bead.

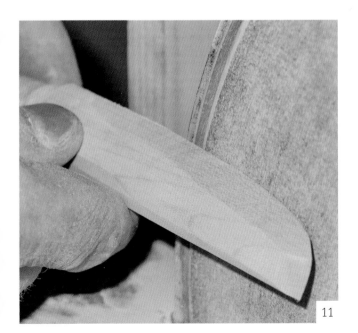

11

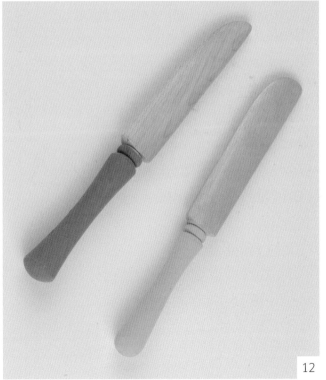

12

11 Use a disc sander to shape the blade as you choose. Once shaped, check to make sure there are no sharp edges. I rounded the edges over, so that they cannot cut or splinter.

12 Apply your choice of color and finish. I colored the handles and one of the blade sections with toy-safe pens.

To add the finishing touches to the tea party, why not make some attractive wooden plates on which to display the food? You can expand upon the standard plate design by creating options such as a pedestal plate for the sponge cake or a tiered cake stand that uses three plates to showcase a variety of goodies.

Plate

Tools and materials

PPE: facemask/respirator

Drive spur and revolving center

Chuck

Non-slip router mat and friction drive/faceplate

Bowl gouge

Thin parting tool

Angled scraper or skew chisel

Bead forming tool

Abrasives, 120–400 grit

Drill and large sanding arbor

Primer

Gloss paint

Whatever version of the plate you wish to create, you will need to start with the basic method. Just alter the sizes a little to suit your final design. Plates are created from faceplate-grain oriented wood, to make them strong and to avoid the short grain that can easily fracture across. Sycamore, beech, birch, walnut, maple and fruitwoods would be ideal for this.

For a standard plate to be stable when in use, the base – the area on which the bowl is supported – needs to be a minimum of one third of the overall diameter. If the plate is very shallow, you can take this to one half as you will not easily be able to see the base when the plate is viewed on the table.

I didn't want any holes in my plates. So, I opted to mount flat discs of wood between centers with a piece of non-slip router mat between the wood and the wastewood friction drive/faceplate at the headstock end. This allowed me to turn the underside of the plate first. You could use a screw chuck with a short screw to mount the blank, or a faceplate with short screws. All options provide security, but because I always use the tailstock where I can (and it marks the base so I can later perfectly centralize the plate for cleaning off the underside), this is a fast and safe mounting method as long as the wood is flat.

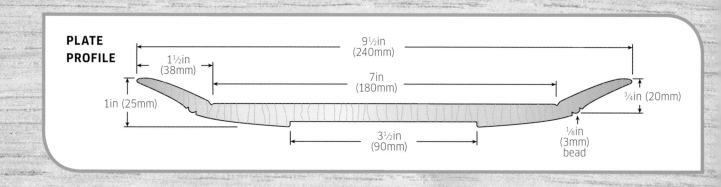

PLATE PROFILE

9½in (240mm)
1½in (38mm)
1in (25mm)
7in (180mm)
¾in (20mm)
3½in (90mm)
⅛in (3mm) bead

1

2

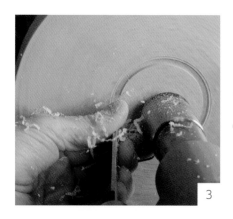

3

1 Mount flat discs of wood between centers, with a piece of non-slip router mat between the wood and the friction drive – a faceplate in this case.

2 Once the piece is secure between centers, use a bowl gouge with a swept-back grind and a pull cut with no bevel rubbing to get the surface flat. Note that the flute is pointing to about 10 o'clock, and the cut is occurring on the lower wing.

3 Once the surface is more or less flat, use a thin parting tool to cut at the width of the spigot or recess required. This cut is 3/16 in. (5mm) deep.

4

5

4 Use a combination of gouge and angled scraper or skew to recess the inner section to the depth required. Stop short, of course, of the ring center you are using. Shape the outer cove-type edge of the plate.

5 Refine the lower body shape, leaving enough flat area for the base width of the plate being turned. To delineate the lower body section from the outer cove-type section, cut a ¹/₈-in. (3mm) bead with a bead forming tool. This provides a visual and tactile break on the plate. You can use a scraper, gouge or parting tool to create the bead if you prefer.

6 I decided to add a bead to the outer area of the base, as well. So, we have a flat base area with a hollow inner section (note the slight cove on the outer area of the recess cut). There is still a ⅛-in. (3mm) flat section for my chuck jaws to grip on to. The lower body curve meets another bead, then comes the outward sweeping cove-type section. When the plate is viewed from the side, the body form is effectively a flattened ogee (S-curve) shape before it meets the bead of the base.

7 When it is shaped to your satisfaction, sand the piece. Be careful not to flatten off the tops of the cut beads.

8 Remove the piece from the lathe and mount it on your chuck. Use the bowl gouge to first cut the inner rim section. I worked down in stages. Even though the wood is 'dry', it will move due to tension release if I cut too deeply before finishing off the topmost section.

9 Cut down one step, then another. Finish the first, then cut the third. Finish the second, and so on, until you reach the depth required. Note that the tailstock is used for support until it gets in the way at the very center.

10 You can see now how the outer wall section mimics the shape, but thickens off slightly at the lower inner section, at the upsweep. The lower inner section of the plate should be absolutely flat.

PLATE **169**

11 To ensure the lower inner section was flat, I used the angled scraper to refine it. You could use a skew on its side, if you need to.

12 Once the section is flat, sand the areas you can reach while the tailstock is still in place.

13 Remove the tailstock and use the gouge to remove the nub of wood that was left under the ring center.

14 Blend in the two areas. A drill with a large sanding arbor works well for this.

15 Once complete, I decided to use the sanding arbor in the drill to soften the previously cut cove on the outer chucking area. This does away with the need to reverse mount the piece between centers and clean up the recess.

16 Apply your choice of color and finish. I first applied a coat of prime. Over this, I applied a coat of white paint, followed by a colored gloss paint on the upper outer and inner curved areas.

Variation: Tiered cake stand

A tiered cake stand requires a modification of the basic plate design, with three plates reducing in diameter as you go up. You need to drill a hole centrally in the lowest, widest plate about halfway though the center depth. The other two plates need a hole drilled all the way though their centers. The holes enable support pedestals to be inserted. Note that the lower support is the tallest, the middle one shorter and slightly narrower, and the top support is just a knob to hold for additional support when carrying the cake stand.

It is best to drill the holes before shaping the plates, then you can mount these on screw chucks to turn the underside, with a spigot or recess. Then, mount the bowl in a chuck to turn the top face of the plate (A). Fit the plate between centers using a jam chuck with a spigot cut the same size as the drilled hole, so you have perfect centralization while turning off and adjusting the spigot or recess (B).

Variation: Pedestal bowl

If you want to create a pedestal bowl, you don't need the flat base section to be quite as wide. Just cut a base that will lock into the recess, being mindful that the lower base area should be wider than the widest part that sits against the plate. Do check the appearance of the two pieces to make sure they look balanced for stability and proportion before gluing them together.

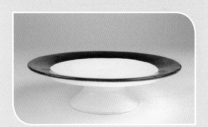

PLATE   **171**

With four teacups and four matching saucers, we are well prepared for that essential oil that turns the wheels of any tea party – the tea! This teacup is based on a stylized design, which has no handle so that it is easy to make and very robust, able to withstand hours of play.

Teacups and saucers

Tools and materials

PPE: facemask/respirator

Drive spur, overshield and revolving center

Chuck

Calipers

Beading and parting tool

Spindle roughing gouge or spindle gouge

Skew chisel

Vernier calipers

Round-nose or French curve scraper

Abrasives, 120–400 grit

Bowl gouge

Angled scraper

Thin parting tool

Cordless drill and ½ in. (13mm) drum sander

Paper towel

Primer

Gloss paint

The cup is a spindle-grain project, for which I used maple (*Acer* sp.). The saucer, like the Plate project, is a bowl-grain project. Given the saucer's size, you can turn it as you would any single bowl, plate or platter project where the wood is first mounted on a faceplate or screw chuck, the back is turned and, once shaped and sanded, reversed, held in a chuck and then the top face turned and sanded. But here, due to the small size of the saucer I will use a faster and easier method used for batch production of smaller plate-like items. Once again, most dense close-grained hardwoods would work well for this project.

This is a great project for practicing your tool control and copy turning skills. You need all the matching parts to be as close to the same size as possible. Use calipers and other such measuring devices to help you achieve the desired accuracy.

Variant designs of cups with handles have been around for millennia. However, handles can be fragile and prone to breakage on objects this small. I didn't want those risks and hazards, which could potentially make them dangerous for a young child to play with, so I chose a more Asian-style cup that fits in the hand nicely, is easy to create and looks good. Do some research into the styles of items you like and try and integrate these aspects into your work.

CUP PROFILE

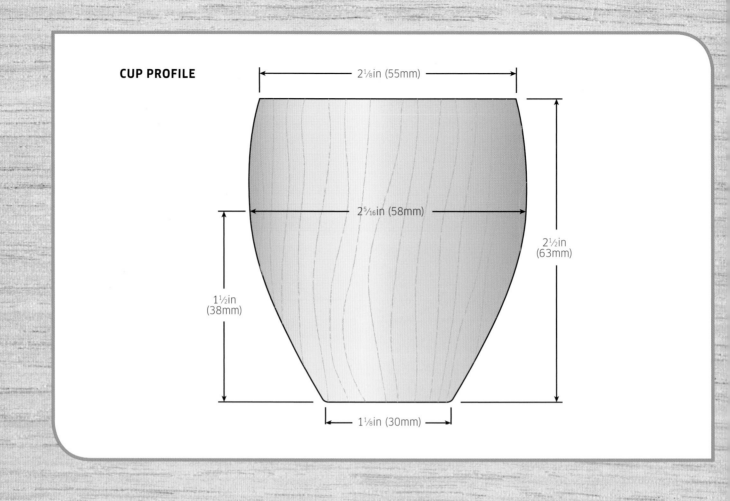

2⅛in (55mm)

2⁵⁄₁₆in (58mm)

2½in (63mm)

1½in (38mm)

1⅛in (30mm)

MAKING THE CUPS

1 Mount a smoothed-down cylinder of wood in the chuck. I used an offcut of maple from the Cupcake project. The diameter needs reducing for this project, so use calipers set to ¹⁄₁₆ in. (1.5mm) bigger than the required diameter to give a bit of adjustment room in case of torn grain and tool control errors. With a beading and parting tool, cut to the width set by the calipers.

1

2

2 Use a spindle roughing gouge or spindle gouge to create a cylinder of the correct width, matching the parting cut created by the beading and parting tool. Then, using the beading and parting tool, make a cut in an area that leaves more than enough wood to turn the cup to the required length. Turn to a minimum diameter of 1⅛ in. (30mm) – no less, or you will not have the stability required to turn the inside of the cup or the required width for the base of the cup.

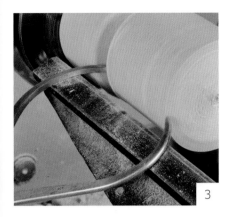

3 Now set the calipers to the required depth of the cup, plus $1/16$ in. (1.5mm) to allow for clean up and sanding. Make cuts using the beading and parting tool until you achieve the depth required.

4 Use the spindle gouge to roughly shape the outside of the teacup.

5 When you are getting close to the required shape, pay particular attention to the curvature and the widest part of the top half of the cup. You won't be able to achieve the correct curve for the bottom just yet, as that area is thicker than you need at the moment.

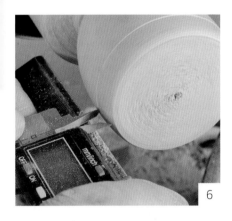

6 When you are happy with the shape of the teacup, measure and mark the position for the incised band. Depending on how deeply you want to mark the position, use the point of a skew to incise the top and bottom boundary with a V cut. Working with vernier calipers did this beautifully for me. This will provide an anti-bleed barrier or a clear boundary to work to if you want to color the teacup.

7 Using the spindle gouge with the handle low, create a delicate, peeling, shear cut and clean up the top surface.

8 Set the rest at a height that allows you to have the spindle gouge horizontal and the tip dead on center. With the flute pointing at the 10 o'clock position, push the gouge into the dead center of the cup and effectively drill in about $3/8$ in. (10mm). Then, extract the blade.

9

10

11

9 With the spindle gouge presented ³/₁₆ in. (5mm) into the center hole, use the same flute presentation angle as before to pull the blade across and cut on the lower wing until you reach just shy of the required inner width.

10 Repeat this process, working ever deeper until you get almost to the required depth.

11 Using a suitably shaped round-nose or French curve scraper, refine the inner section to the shape required. To minimize catches, I set the rest higher so that the cutting edge is always lower than the handle.

12

13

12 When you are happy with the shape, sand the inner section, rim and top section of the cup to a fine finish.

13 Refine the lower section as necessary to attain the correct diameter for the bottom area, and clean up with abrasives before parting off. I found it easiest to make all four cups first and then set them to one side before moving on to the saucers.

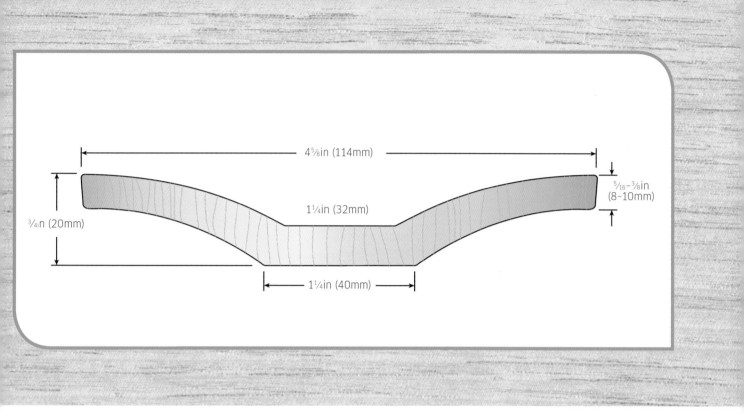

4⅝in (114mm)

1¼in (32mm)

¾in (20mm)

⁵⁄₁₆–³⁄₈in (8–10mm)

1¼in (40mm)

MAKING THE SAUCERS

1 For the saucers, I began by mounting a bowl blank between centers. A screw hole would waste too much wood.

2 You only need to cut a small spigot on the tailstock end to hold the piece for creating the saucers. Using a bowl gouge with a swept-back wing, make a pull cut to clean up the face. Then, use a push cut to create the spigot – one about ¼ in. (6mm) deep is fine. Follow this with a pull or push cut to make the rest of the surface flat.

3

4

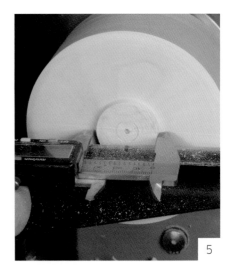

5

3 My blank was too wide, and it is likely that the one you are using is not exactly the right size. So, clean up the edge until you attain the required diameter.

4 It is best to work from both ends of the blank to minimize the risk of fracturing the top or bottom corners.

5 When you reach the correct width, remove the wood from between centers and mount the piece in your chuck. Use a push cut with the bowl gouge to clean up the face. Using another push cut, create the curved top rim section of the saucer. Stop short of the center, where you will need to create a recessed area in which the cup will sit. The cut creates a little spigot, which, when measured and adjusted for size, will be the same size as that required for the recess.

6

7

6 Using the beading and parting tool, make a series of plunge cuts following the width of the spigot. Cut to the depth required for the saucer.

7 When the recess is the correct depth and size, use the corner of the skew or an angled scraper to incise a slight V at the widest part of the recess. Then, clean up the outer area.

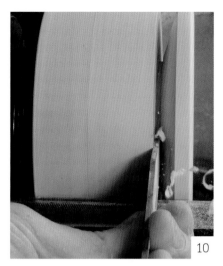

8 When you are happy with the profile of the top, sand to a fine finish. Now mark the overall depth required for the saucer: the vernier calipers work well for this.

9 Using a parting tool (this is a thin one to minimize waste), part down just wider than the base thickness required.

10 With the thin parting tool, part in at an angle to create a chamfered profile on the back that meets up with your previous parting cut. Then, part the piece off.

11 Set the piece aside and begin the process again by shaping the top face of the next saucer.

12 Shape the top curved face and repeat steps 1 to 11 until you have four saucers ready for work on the bases. At this point, you can choose to mount them sequentially between centers or in a jam chuck, and refine the underneath of each saucer. I used a between-centers method to clean them up, as shown in steps 13 to 18.

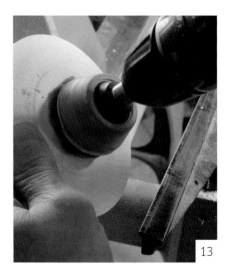

13

14

13 Begin by sanding the base of the first piece.

14 Now, use either a jam chuck with a recess the right size to accept the saucer; or a between-centers friction drive method, where some form of overshield with a flat front face that slides over your revolving center is used to hold the wood in place. The overshield or a dedicated flat-end revolving center is necessary so that there are no sharp bits to bite into the previously sanded bottom of the saucer.

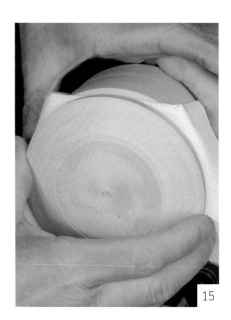

15

16

15 Place paper towel over your just-shaped saucer top. Bring up the previous saucer and place the finished face against the paper towel.

16 Bring up the tailstock and revolving center fitted with the overshield – this one is a plastic bottle cap stuffed with tissue paper, but other non-marking materials could be used to good effect – and centralize the piece.

17 Not much pressure is required to keep the work in place, but you might need to gently tap the piece to centralize it properly. When secure, work at about 600rpm for this diameter and use a pull cut to form the shape required. Then, sand it.

18 When you have finished sanding, remove the tailstock and saucer. You should see no damage from the overshield. I would not use this method on larger work, preferring instead the security of a ring center bite. A recessed jam chuck would minimize the risk of knocking it off center and (depending on how tight the fit) could be used with or without tailstock center support.

19 Apply your choice of color and finish. I gave the cups and saucers a coat of primer and then used white gloss. This was finished with colored gloss paint on the inner recess and edge of the saucer, and on the band of the cups.

No tea party would be complete without a teapot. Making the teapot large adds to its appeal, but suitable solid wood can be very expensive and hard to source. So, in order to reduce the cost of making the teapot while ensuring I still had a dimensionally stable piece of material, I laminated together sheets of high quality birch-faced ply.

Teapot

Tools and materials

PPE: facemask/respirator

Drive spur and revolving center

Chuck

Screw chuck or screw chuck attachment

Bowl gouge

Beading and parting tool

Round-nose or French curve scraper

Angled scraper or skew chisel

Cordless drill and sanding arbor

Forceps or sanding ball (optional, depending on teapot shape)

Abrasives, 120–400 grit

Thin parting tool

Bead forming tool, ¾ in. (20mm)

Drill bit, ¼ in. (6mm), to suit your screw chuck

Panel pins

¼-in. (6mm) dowel

Adhesive – aliphatic resin or PVA

Primer

Gloss paint

There are pros and cons to using laminated birch-faced ply. On the one hand, the ply can – without due care – pick and pluck when turning. It leaves holes, gaps and roughened surfaces that need filling and sanding heavily, and it is very dusty to turn. Like some hardwoods, it can also be heavy if left in too thick a section. On the other hand, it is dimensionally stable to use, is cheaper than solid wood and stronger than some woods. The other plus is that you can use your standard turning tools to shape it.

Laminated birch-faced ply will also allow you to make a teapot handle and spout that will not (or, at least, should not, if large enough and bonded correctly!) break. Ply has a lot going for it but it must be used sensitively and with due consideration for the problems associated with its use.

I laminated up one piece for the body and one for the lid. You could laminate up just one longer piece, but the lid is a lot smaller than the teapot and I don't like waste. But of course how you create yours is entirely up to you.

I made four prototypes from solid wood before deciding on the laminated ply version. In all cases I ended up with breakages on the 'solid' wood versions for some reason. As with everything you make, try things out so you can find out the best way for you.

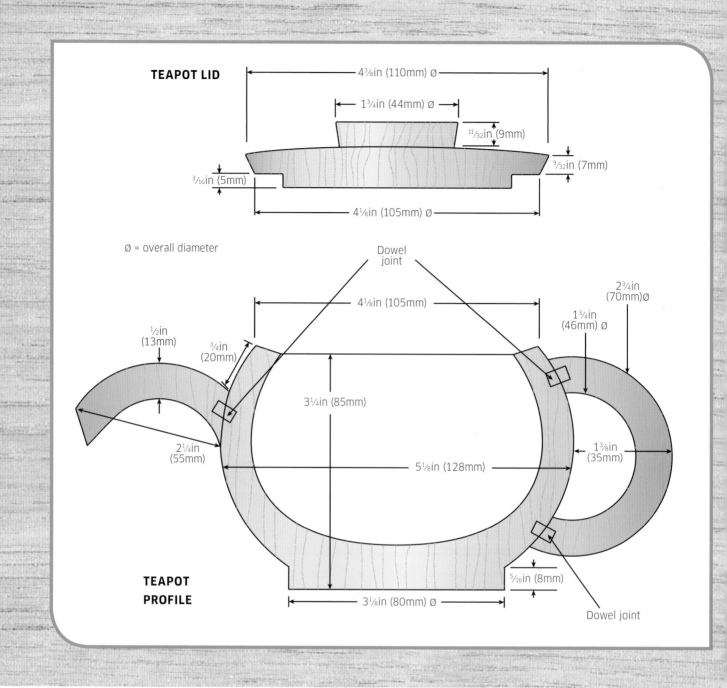

TEAPOT LID

4³⁄₈in (110mm) Ø

1³⁄₄in (44mm) Ø

¹¹⁄₃₂in (9mm)

⁹⁄₃₂in (7mm)

³⁄₁₆in (5mm)

4¹⁄₈in (105mm) Ø

Ø = overall diameter

Dowel joint

4¹⁄₈in (105mm)

2³⁄₄in (70mm)Ø

1³⁄₄in (46mm) Ø

½in (13mm)

¾in (20mm)

3¹⁄₄in (85mm)

1³⁄₈in (35mm)

2¹⁄₄in (55mm)

5¹⁄₈in (128mm)

TEAPOT PROFILE

5⁄₁₆in (8mm)

3¹⁄₈in (80mm) Ø

Dowel joint

1 You can mount the block of ply on a screw chuck or faceplate, but I decided to mount it between centers and cut a recess at the tailstock end. Then, I removed the piece and mounted it on my chuck. It is a heavy piece, so get the support of the chuck to hold it as soon as you can. Once the block is secure you can start shaping the teapot. Note how the tailstock is used for support.

1

2

3

4

2 The tailstock end will form the bottom of the teapot. Use a bowl gouge to roughly shape this lower area and cut the base section. The base outer edge needs to be a minimum 40 per cent of the overall width for stability. I decided to have a recess, which allowed me to create a slight upstand for the base. Do not make this wall too thick, otherwise the expansion of the chuck jaws could shear the joint of the laminates. Using a beading and parting tool, you can create the recess in the base quite easily.

3 When you have shaped the lower outside section of the teapot – with the widest part about two-thirds of the way up from the base section – you can remove the piece from the lathe. Reverse it and mount it on the chuck using the recess you have just cut. Refine the top outer curve to meet the widest part. An angled scraper or skew on its side in scraping mode might help to refine the shape.

4 The grain direction is all over the place, but treat it like any other bowl work. Cut from smallest to largest on the outside. When you are happy with the outside, move on to the inside and cut from largest to smallest. The undercut required to go from the width of the opening to the widest part would technically, in bowl grain, be going against the grain. Using a round-nose or French curve scraper might help to refine the shape.

5

5 When you have the correct inner shape, sand it. Do not stick your fingers inside. Round off all the outer edges and then sand the top and inner sections. Using a drill with an arbor, you might be able to reach everything, depending on shape and depth. Alternatively, something like a sanding ball or forceps will hold abrasive and will reach inside this shape. Do not ever hold forceps with your fingers in the finger holes when sanding.

6

6 Once smooth, remove the piece. Now, either mount the top opening on a jam chuck, or expand the jaws into the opening to gently hold the teapot. Refine the outer section and the base detail. I chose to make the teapot quite squat. When you are happy with the refinements, sand the piece and remove from the lathe.

7 Mount the lid section between centers. Using the bowl gouge, make a clean cylinder with a spigot and mount it in your chuck. Now, shape what will be the underside of the lid, with a spigot to suit the opening of the teapot. Note how the ply laminations are oriented so that this appears like a spindle-grain project. I am still, however, working it like a bowl-grain project.

8 Once you have the right spigot shape and flange, cut so that the lid will sit nicely in the teapot. Sand the underside.

9 Reverse mount the lid in your chuck and gently lock on to the spigot you have cut, using tissue paper to minimize marking. A recessed jam chuck would work well, too. Refine the shape of the lid top, creating a knob in the center.

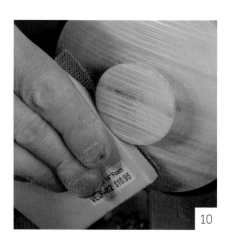

10 Refine the shape of the outer edge. When satisfied with this, sand it smooth.

11 Now we need to create the teapot handle and spout. For this, I laminated up another block of ply from which a ring needed to be cut. Drill your blank with a hole to suit your screw chuck and mount it on. Clean up the sides, but don't make it too narrow.

12 With the lathe stationary, place the teapot against the ply. Look to see what diameter you will need for a handle of the right size. This will be created from a section of the ring.

13 When you are happy with the diameter, plunge cut with a thin parting tool into the top face of the ply. Cut to about ³/₄ in. (20mm) deep, about ³/₄ in. (20mm) in from the outer edge. Use a gouge or bead forming tool to shape the outer edge of the ring, creating a nice bead shape ³/₄ in. (20mm) wide. Once shaped and sanded, use the parting tool to part the ring at the lowest part of the outer bead nearest the chuck. You should meet the inner cut, which will make the ring release nicely.

14 Now you need to cut the ring to create what will be the spout and the handle. You can see how the ring is cut. When cut, sand both pieces and adjust the cuts – especially the spout – so that you get a nice fit against the body curve.

15 Drill a hole in each end of the handle and another in the spout, where they meet the body of the teapot, to suit panel pins. In these holes, fit panel pins and then use these to indent the correct seating positions of the handle and spout on the teapot. Remove the pins, and drill ¹/₄-in. (6mm) holes to accept small dowels in the spout and handles. Drill corresponding fixing holes in the body of the pot. Glue everything in place.

Apply your choice of color and finish. I used two coats of primer and one coat of white gloss. Adding colored gloss paint to the lid, spout and handle provides the finishing touches for your teapot.

Suppliers

Below is a list of contact details for suppliers and manufacturers whose products I have used in this book. There are many others that I do not have space to mention; you will find them in local directories and woodworking magazines.

UK

Ashley Iles (Edge Tools) Ltd
East Kirkby
Spilsby
Lincs PE23 4DD
Tel: +44 (0)1790 763372
www.ashleyiles.co.uk

Axminster Tools & Machinery
Unit 10
Weycroft Avenue
Axminster
Devon EX13 5PH
Tel: 0800 371822
www.axminster.co.uk

Chestnut Products
PO Box 260
Stowmarket
IP14 9BX
Tel: +44 (0)1473 890118
www.chestnutproducts.co.uk

Crown Hand Tools Ltd
332–334 Coleford Road
Darnall
Sheffield S9 5PH
Tel: +44 (0)1142 612300
www.crownhandtools.ltd.uk

General Finishes UK
Unit 13
Peffermill Parc
25 King's Haugh
Edinburgh EH16 5UY
(by appointment only)
Tel: +44 (0)1316 615553
www.generalfinishes.co.uk

Hamlet Craft Tools
The Forge
Peacock Estate
Livesey Street
Sheffield S6 2BL
Tel: +44 (0)1142 321338
www.hamletcrafttools.co.uk

Henry Taylor Tools Ltd
The Forge
Peacock Estate
Livesey Street
Sheffield S6 2BL
Tel: +44 (0)1142 340282 /
340321
www.henrytaylortools.co.uk

Liberon Waxes Ltd
Learoyd Road
Mountfield Industrial Estate
New Romney
Kent TN28 8XU
Tel: +44 (0)1797 367555
www.liberon.co.uk

Mylands
26 Rothschild Street
London SE27 0HQ
Tel: +44 (0)208 6709161
www.mylands.co.uk

Record Power Ltd
Centenary House
11 Midland Way
Barlborough Links
Chesterfield
Derbyshire S43 4XA
Tel: +44 (0)1246 571 020
www.recordpower.co.uk

Robert Sorby
Athol Road
Sheffield S8 0PA
Tel: +44 (0)1142 250700
www.robert-sorby.co.uk

Rustins Limited
Drayton Works
Waterloo Road
London
NW2 7TX
Tel: +44 (0)20 8450 4666
www.rustins.eu

Stiles & Bates
Upper Farm
Church Hill
Sutton
Dover
Kent CT15 5DF
Tel: +44 (0)1304 366360
www.stilesandbates.co.uk

The ToolPost
Unit 7, Hawksworth
Southmead Industrial Park
Didcot
Oxfordshire OX11 7HR
Tel: +44 (0)1235 511101
www.toolpost.co.uk

Turners Retreat
The Woodworkers Source
Faraday Close
Harworth
Notts DN11 8RU
Tel: +44 (0)1302 744344
www.turners-retreat.co.uk

Yandle & Sons Ltd
Hurst Works
Martock
Somerset TA12 6JU
Tel: +44 (0)1935 822207
www.yandles.co.uk

AUSTRALIA

Vicmarc Machinery

52 Grice Street

Clontarf

Queensland 4019

Tel: +61 (0)7 3284 3103

www.vicmarc.com

CANADA

Oneway Manufacturing

Unit 1, 291 Griffith Road

Stratford

Ontario N5A 6S4

Toll-free (USA and Canada only):

1-800-565-7288

www.oneway.ca

USA

Craft Supplies USA

1287 E 1120 S

Provo, UT 84606

Tel: 1-800-551-8876

www.woodturnerscatalog.com

Packard Woodworks Inc

215 S Trade Street

Tryon, NC 28782

Tel: 1-828-859-6762

Toll-free (USA and Canada only):

1-800-683-8876

www.packardwoodworks.com

Thompson Lathe Tools

Doug Thompson

5479 Columbia Road

N. Olmsted, OH 44070

Tel: 1-440-241-6360

www.thompsonlathetools.com

Woodcraft Supply LLC

PO Box 1686

Parkersburg, WV 26102-1686

Tel: 1-304-428-4866

Toll-free (USA and Canada only):

1-800-225-1153

www.woodcraft.com

Acknowledgments

There are many aspects, including the help of others, that need to come together in order to make a book. I would like to give special thanks to the following people for their kind help and support: **Walter Hall** and **Chris West** for reading the book and making sure I hadn't missed out anything and that my comments made sense; **David Button** for allowing me to raid his lumber store for some materials; **Lesley Churton** for the inspiration for the hedgehog project; **Stuart King** for his help and advice and with photos for the ring/hoop-turned toys project; **Sara Harper** for her patience as the book editor – it is no easy task putting books together.

I would also like to thank the following companies for their help:

Ashley Iles (Edge Tools) Ltd www.ashleyiles.co.uk

Axminster Tools & Machinery www.axminster.co.uk

David Bates www.stilesandbates.co.uk

Chestnut Products www.chestnutproducts.co.uk

Crown Hand Tools www.crownhandtools.ltd.uk

Drechselzentrum Erzegebirge (Steiner) www.drechselzentrum.de

Henry Taylor Tools Ltd www.henrytaylortools.co.uk

Paul Howard www.paulhowardwoodturner.co.uk

Record Power www.recordpower.co.uk

Robert Sorby www.robert-sorby.co.uk

Simon Hope www.hopewoodturning.co.uk

The ToolPost www.toolpost.co.uk

Turners Retreat www.turners-retreat.co.uk

Picture credits

Axminster Power Tool Centre (p. 13, middle); Lesley Churton (p. 28); Stuart King (p. 112), Record Power Ltd (p. 13, top).

About the author

Mark Baker has always been fascinated by wood. His father was a carpenter and joiner and, on leaving school, Mark served a five-year apprenticeship working for a local building firm, which included restoration work. Mark has also helped set up an industrial workshop for autistic adults and he has worked for a major manufacturer of woodturning tools in the UK. He is now the editor of *Woodturning* magazine and the group editor of all GMC Publications woodworking magazines. Previous books include *Woodturning Projects: A Workshop Guide to Shapes*; *Wood for Woodturners*; *Wood Turning: A Craftman's Guide* and *Weekend Woodturning Projects*, all published by GMC Publications.

Imperial-Metric Conversions

Note that some conversions have been rounded up, so when measuring, please ensure that you follow EITHER the imperial OR the metric system throughout. Do not mix the two.

Imperial	Metric		Imperial	Metric		Imperial	Metric		Imperial	Metric
5/64 in.	2mm		15/16 in.	24mm		3¾ in.	95mm		7¼ in.	185mm
1/8 in.	3mm		1 in.	25mm		4 in.	100mm		7½ in.	190mm
5/32 in.	4mm		1⅛ in.	30mm		4⅛ in.	105mm		7¾ in.	195mm
3/16 in.	5mm		1¼ in.	32mm		4¼ in.	107mm		8 in.	200mm
¼ in.	6mm		1⅜ in.	35mm		4⅜ in.	110mm		8¼ in.	210mm
9/32 in.	7mm		1½ in.	38mm		4½ in.	115mm		8½ in.	215mm
5/16 in.	8mm		1⅝ in.	40mm		4¾ in.	120mm		8¾ in.	220mm
11/32 in.	9mm		1¾ in.	45mm		5 in.	125mm		9 in.	230mm
⅜ in.	10mm		2 in.	50mm		5⅛ in.	130mm		9¼ in.	235mm
7/16 in.	11mm		2⅛ in.	52mm		5¼ in.	135mm		9½ in.	240mm
½ in.	13mm		2¼ in.	55mm		5½ in.	140mm		9¾ in.	250mm
9/16 in.	15mm		2⅜ in.	60mm		5¾ in.	145mm		10 in.	255mm
⅝ in.	16mm		2½ in.	63mm		6 in.	150mm		10⅛ in.	257mm
11/16 in.	17mm		2⅝ in.	65mm		6⅛ in.	155mm		11 in.	280mm
23/32 in.	18mm		2¾ in.	70mm		6¼ in.	160mm		12 in.	305mm
¾ in.	20mm		3 in.	75mm		6½ in.	165mm		13 in.	330mm
13/16 in.	21mm		3⅛ in.	80mm		6¾ in.	170mm		14 in.	355mm
⅞ in.	22mm		3¼ in.	85mm		6⅞ in.	178mm			
29/32 in.	23mm		3½ in.	90mm		7 in.	180mm			

Index

To order a book, or to request a catalog, contact:
The Taunton Press, Inc.
63 South Main Street, P.O. Box 5506
Newtown, CT 06470-5506
Tel: (800) 888-8286
www.tauntonstore.com